Brewing Bliss: Tea Gardening Unveiled for Beginners

A Green Thumb's Guide to Growing Your Own Tea Sanctuary

Adrian Wells

Table of Contents

INTRODUCTION

Welcome to "Brewing Bliss: Tea Gardening Unveiled for Beginners – A Green Thumb's Guide to Growing Your Own Tea Sanctuary." In the hustle and bustle of modern life, the idea of cultivating your own tea garden offers a refreshing escape and a journey into the soothing realm of tea culture. This comprehensive guide is designed for beginners eager to embark on the enriching adventure of tea gardening, providing insights into the art of nurturing tea plants and creating a personal sanctuary for tea enthusiasts.

Tea, with its rich cultural history and diverse flavors, has long been cherished as more than just a beverage. "Brewing Bliss" invites you to explore the joy of growing your own tea, from selecting the perfect tea varieties to crafting a serene tea corner where you can savor the fruits of your labor. Whether you're a gardening novice or a seasoned green thumb, this guide will equip you with the knowledge and skills needed to cultivate a thriving tea garden right at home.

In the opening chapters, we'll delve into the basics of tea gardening, demystifying the world of tea varieties and guiding you in selecting the most suitable plants for your unique space. As we progress, you'll learn the art of planning and designing your tea sanctuary, understanding the nuances of soil preparation, and mastering the delicate balance of watering, fertilizing, and pest control.

As you nurture your tea plants from seeds or seedlings to flourishing bushes, "Brewing Bliss" will lead you through the seasons, from the anticipation of the first harvest to the joy of processing your own tea leaves. Beyond the garden, we'll explore the creation of a tranquil tea space, the art of blending flavors, and the health benefits associated with homegrown teas.

Join us on this delightful journey into the world of tea gardening. Whether you dream of cultivating a small balcony garden or transforming your backyard into a tea haven, "Brewing Bliss" is your comprehensive guide to achieving the perfect blend of nature, relaxation, and the simple pleasure of a freshly brewed cup of homegrown tea.

CHAPTER I

The Basics of Tea Gardening

Understanding Tea Varieties

Tea, the world's second-most beverage after water, has a rich tapestry of flavors and aromas woven through the diverse varieties of Camellia sinensis, the tea plant. This botanical marvel has resulted in the development of a remarkable spectrum of tea types, each differentiated by its distinctive processing methods, terroir, and leaf qualities. To get started on the path to developing an appreciation for tea, it is necessary to become familiar with the subtleties of the various types of tea, which include black, green, oolong, white, and pu-erh teas, for example.

During the process of oxidation, black tea, distinguished by its robust flavor and deep amber color, goes through the entire process. A rich and full-bodied cup is produced due to the leaves being withered, rolled, oxidized, and burnt to stop the oxidation process. There are many different types of black tea, but some more popular ones include Assam, Darjeeling, and Ceylon. Each variety has a unique flavor profile influenced by the local growing region.

Green tea, a stark contrast to black tea, is celebrated for its fresh, grassy notes. The leaves undergo minimal oxidation, preserving their natural green hue and imparting a delicate flavor. Green tea has a spectrum of flavors, from bright and vegetal to savory and umami. Imagine sipping on a cup of Sencha with its balanced sweetness and bitterness, Matcha with its rich, creamy texture, or Dragon Well with its nutty, buttery notes.

As a result of the leaves partially oxidized, oolong tea is a type of tea that falls somewhere between black tea and green tea. It is well-recognized that this genre is characterized by its intricate flavor profiles, ranging from fruity and floral to creamy and toasted. The skilled artistry and precise processing processes characteristic of oolong teas are displayed in the oolongs of Tie Guan Yin, Dong Ding, and Phoenix Mountain.

Compared to other types of tea, white tea undergoes the least amount of processing, which results in minor oxidation and preserves the natural appearance of the tea leaves. Silver Needle and Bai Mu Dan are two white teas that give a delicate and refined sipping experience. These teas have a flavor profile that is subtle and nuanced. The processing carried out delicately enables the genuine essence of the tea plant to be revealed.

Pu-erh tea, which is native to the Yunnan province of China, is subjected to a one-of-a-kind fermentation and aging process, which ultimately leaves it with a flavor that is distinctively earthy and frequently powerful. These post-fermented teas are crushed into cakes or bricks, with Sheng pu-erh (raw) and Shou pu-erh (ripe) pu-erh signifying different processing procedures. The flavor of pu-erh becomes more complex over time, which is one of the reasons why tea collectors and enthusiasts look for it.

In addition to the conventional classifications, the world of tea is continuously undergoing development with the introduction of revolutionary mixes, herbal infusions, and artisanal creations. Because they are not derived from Camellia sinensis, technically, authentic herbal teas offer various flavors and health advantages. A few examples of popular herbal infusions are chamomile, peppermint, and hibiscus, each of which is lauded for its distinctive qualities.

Terroir, which refers to the specific environmental conditions that impact the cultivation of tea, is an essential component in determining the flavor profiles of various types of tea. A number of factors contribute to the final brew's specific qualities, including the height, climate, soil composition, and even the orientation of the plantation. Consequently, teas originating from Assam in India have the potential to exhibit malty and robust notes, while teas originating from the highlands of Taiwan may display flowery and creamy attributes.

Tea types are appreciated not just for their flavor but also for the cultural traditions and rituals that they represent. The elaborate tea ceremony practiced in Japan is a celebration of the preparation and eating of Matcha, a powdered form of green tea. With gong fu cha, also known as the art of brewing tea, being a renowned activity in China, tea drinking is firmly ingrained in the country's culture daily. The British have ways of doing things, and one of those ways is through their afternoon tea rituals, which highlight the sophistication of black tea served with scones and clotted cream.

In conclusion, gaining an awareness of the various types of tea involves an investigation into the multiple ways Camellia sinensis can be expressed, as well as the intricate craftsmanship responsible for transforming the leaves into a wide variety of flavors and scents. The intensity of black teas and the subtlety of white teas are just two examples of the many varieties of tea that urge us to taste the richness of a beverage that is not limited by national boundaries or cultural norms. Tea is an elixir that has stood the test of time and continues to captivate and inspire people, regardless of whether it is consumed in solitude for its meditative properties or in the company of others.

Selecting the Right Tea Plants

Embarking on the journey of tea gardening is a venture into the world of Camellia sinensis, the venerable tea plant that has captivated humanity for centuries. The importance of carefully selecting tea plants suited to your environment, space, and individual preferences cannot be overstated when it comes to the success of your tea garden. Whether the robust Assam or the delicate Dragon Well, each variety of tea has its own set of qualities and requirements. Because of this, selecting the appropriate tea plants is an essential stage in the process of developing a flourishing tea sanctuary.

When picking tea plants, the first and most important factor is to evaluate the area's climate. Camellia sinensis is a hardy and versatile plant, so different kinds of plants flourish in different environments. For instance, if you live in a region with a warmer climate, the Assam type, which is well-known for having a robust and malty flavor, would be an excellent option for you. On the other hand, if the temperature in your region is lower, a tea plant such as the robust Russian Caravan is more suitable for your climate. To guarantee that you select tea plants that will survive and thrive in their environment, it is essential to have a thorough understanding of the intricacies of your local climate.

Your choice of tea plants will also be impacted by the dimensions of your tea garden and the amount of available space. The cultivation of Camellia sinensis can occur in various environments, ranging from compact containers on a balcony to enormous gardens. Close types, such as the Chinese plant Xiao Zhong or the Japanese Shizu-Inzatsu 131, are perfect for limited settings. This makes it possible for even people with modest gardening areas to experience the enjoyment of drinking tea that originated from their garden. On the other hand, larger tea bushes, such as Camellia sinensis var. sinensis, which is well-known for its adaptability in processing many varieties of tea, can be accommodated if sufficient space is available.

It would also help to consider the reason for your tea garden. What are your goals for cultivating tea? Are you interested in producing personalized mixes, developing tea for its leaves, or creating a space conducive to meditation for tea ceremonies? There are numerous types of tea, each of which is best suited for a particular purpose. If you want to try various flavors and experiment with different kinds of tea, a flexible cultivar such as Camellia sinensis var. sinensis would be the best option. Alternatively, if you are drawn to the peaceful ritual of matcha preparation, the Tencha cultivar, which is essential for matcha manufacturing and thrives in the shade, could be an ideal choice.

To make an informed decision, it is essential to have a solid understanding of the features of the various tea plant varieties. Camellia sinensis var. sinensis and Camellia sinensis var. assamica are the principal subspecies used to classify the tea plant into their respective categories. The former variety, which has its roots in China, is distinguished by its smaller leaves and is typically linked with flavors that are easier to identify. This kind, indigenous to the Assam region of India, is characterized by more giant leaves and tends to produce bolder and more robust teas. The subspecies are further subdivided into many cultivars, each with distinct flavor subtleties and specific requirements for cultivation.

The Camellia sinensis var. sinensis cultivar provides a wide range of possibilities for individuals looking for a tea plant that is adaptable and easy to care for. It is well known that certain varieties, such as Fuding Da Bai and Bai Ye, play a significant role in the production of white teas with subtle and complex flavors. Longjing and Mao Feng are highly regarded green tea varieties that are lauded for their fragrant and vegetal characteristics. Wuyi Rock Oolong, a cultivar that belongs to the category of oolong tea, exemplifies the diversity within this partially oxidized group by showing a variety of flavors ranging from flowery to toasted.

As an alternative, the Camellia sinensis var. assamica variety, characterized by its giant leaves, is frequently chosen for black teas. The cultivars Assam and Yunnan are particularly notable in this subspecies due to their solid and malty characteristics. Additionally, the Puerh cultivar, which plays a significant role in manufacturing fermented and aged pu-erh teas, is a member of this plant subspecies. By understanding the differences between these subspecies and the cultivars that belong to them, you will be able to align the objectives of your tea garden with the inherent qualities of the plants you ultimately select.

It is not only the subspecies and cultivars of tea plants that affect the flavor profile of the harvested leaves but also the age of the tea plants themselves. The softness of young tea leaves, which are frequently referred to as "buds" or "tips," means that they are highly appreciated and typically produce lighter and more delicate teas. The flavor becomes more intense as the leaves undergo the maturation process, contributing to the depth and richness found in many black teas. By understanding the influence of age on flavor, you can customize your tea garden to produce the kinds of tea to your tastes.

In picking tea plants, it is vital to consider the propagation technique that is most suitable for your gardening style and objectives. Growing tea plants can be accomplished through either seeds or cuttings, with each method presenting its unique set of benefits and difficulties. Tea can be produced from seeds, providing a sense of connection to the plant's natural life cycle. However, this method demands patience because the germination process can take several weeks to months. Alternately, beginning with cuttings offers a way of propagation that is both more immediate and more controlled. This method enables you to imitate the features of a tea plant that has been established for a considerable time.

Also affecting the time it takes for your tea plants to mature and become productive is whether to start them from seeds or cuttings. Compared to plants propagated from cuttings, those grown from seeds often require more time to achieve maturity. It is possible that selecting cuttings is the more advantageous option if you are ready to begin collecting your tea leaves as soon as possible rather than waiting until later. If, on the other hand, you will take pleasure in the process of cultivating tea plants from their earliest stages, then beginning with seeds can be an experience that is both pleasant and educational.

Furthermore, to successfully plan and manage your tea garden, it is essential to have a solid understanding of the lifespan of tea plants. There are times of hibernation, flushes of new growth, and harvest seasons typical for tea plants. However, tea plants typically follow an annual cycle. The timing of these phases varies based on the particular type of tea, the temperature of the area, and the conditions in which the tea is grown. Getting acquainted with the lifespan of the tea plants you have selected will allow you to anticipate significant milestones, plan harvests by those milestones, and ensure that your tea garden receives the best possible care throughout the year.

In conclusion, choosing the appropriate tea plants for your garden is a process that requires attention to detail and consideration of a variety of factors, including temperature, space, the intended use of the garden, and individual tastes. Camellia sinensis var. sinensis is known for its delicate appeal, while Camellia sinensis var. assamica is known for its robust vigor. Both of these varieties of Camellia sinensis contribute to the rich tapestry of tastes that define the world of tea. Your tea garden should blossom as you embark on this horticultural journey. It should not only serve as a source of homegrown leaves but also as a sanctuary where the age-old tradition of tea growing can be carried out in harmony with the naturally occurring environment.

Essential Tools and Supplies

Cultivating a tea garden is a rewarding endeavor that requires a thoughtful selection of essential tools and supplies to ensure the health and prosperity of your tea plants. At each stage of the tea growing process, from the preparation of the soil to the harvesting and processing of the tea, specific instruments customized to the particular requirements of Camellia sinensis are required. Understanding and getting the appropriate tools will considerably contribute to the success of your tea garden, regardless of whether you are an experienced gardener seeking to embark on this enjoyable adventure or a newbie just beginning this journey.

The cornerstone of any successful garden is the soil, and when it comes to tea plants, it is of the utmost importance to ensure that the soil has adequate drainage, aeration, and nutritional content. To stir and loosen the soil, a garden spade or shovel is essential for soil preparation. This will make it easier for the roots of the tea plant to enter the soil. It is helpful to have a soil pH tester to determine the acidity or alkalinity of your soil, as tea plants flourish in circumstances that range from slightly acidic to neutral. Additionally, organic waste, such as compost or manure that has been allowed to decompose, serves as an essential soil amendment, boosting fertility and providing needed nutrients for tea production at its highest possible level.

Once the soil has been prepared for the cultivation of tea, a watering can or a mild hose attachment becomes necessary. Camellia sinensis requires a steady moisture supply, particularly during the vegetative phase of its life cycle. It is recommended to water plants from above to imitate the effects of natural rainfall; nevertheless, it is essential to prevent waterlogging, as this might result in root rot. A drip irrigation system may be a more practical choice for more extensive tea gardens because it allows for regulated and targeted watering.

The practice of pruning tea plants regularly is beneficial

for promoting healthy growth and development. When shaping the bushes, eliminating damaged or dead branches, and fostering new growth, pruning shears or scissors are indispensable. The act of pruning not only helps preserve the plant's structure but also promotes air circulation, which in turn reduces the likelihood of illnesses and pests. Furthermore, because tea plants are frequently cultivated for their leaves, good pruning helps to ensure a more abundant harvest.

Because of the importance of seed trays and small pots

for germination and early seedling growth, individuals who cultivate tea from seeds should consider using them. Before they are ready to be transplanted into the garden, the delicate seedlings are placed in these pots, which provide them with a controlled environment. Using a seedling heat mat can also be advantageous because it ensures appropriate temperatures at which the seeds germinate. This is especially true if you start your tea plants inside or in cooler climates.

When transplanting or moving established tea plants,

your hands will be protected from scratches, thorns, and soil if you use a durable pair of gardening gloves. A further benefit of gloves is that they provide insulation throughout the winter months, which helps to keep your hands comfortable while you tend to your tea garden. By wearing appropriate clothing, such as a hat with a wide brim and long sleeves, you can protect yourself from the sun's rays and reduce the potential allergens you are exposed to.

When protecting tea plants in winter, frost cloth or row

coverings are crucial. Their use is essential in areas that experience colder climates or where frost is a concern. These protective materials offer an additional layer of insulation, which shields the plants from the damaging effects of frost and protects them from excessive temperatures. Because tea plants are susceptible to frost, they must receive adequate protection during the winter months. Their survival may be contingent on the care provided during the colder seasons.

A magnifying glass is a valuable tool for analyzing your tea plants' leaves and determining whether there are any potential pest infestations. This allows you to monitor the overall health of your tea plants. This enables prompt action, preventing pests from inflicting severe harm to your tea garden. Early detection allows for immediate intervention. Another essential tool is a gardening journal that is small enough to fit in your pocket. This journal will enable you to record planting dates, growth trends, and any problems you detect. Because of this record, you will have a helpful resource to improve your tea planting techniques in the coming seasons.

When it comes to tea gardening, harvesting is a crucial point in the calendar, and having the appropriate instruments ensures that the harvest will be effective and efficient. The plucking of tea leaves typically involves the use of hand-held pruning shears or scissors. These shears or scissors should be sharp to produce clean cuts without causing any damage to the plant. Harvesting freshly harvested leaves can be made easier with a lightweight basket or cloth bag, which also helps prevent any unwanted bruising or decaying of the leaves. Because tea's flavor profile can change depending on when the leaves are picked, timing is critical during the harvesting process. As a result of the consistent harvesting, new growth is encouraged, which in turn adds to the overall health of the tea plant.

Processing tea leaves at home is a pleasant component of tea gardening. However, specialist tools are required to transform freshly picked tea leaves into a finished beverage. In the process of making oolong teas, a tea rolling machine is frequently utilized since it assists in the release of the essential oils and tastes that are contained inside the leaves. Traditional and tactile techniques of shaping tea leaves can be achieved using a bamboo tea rolling pad, ideal for those who prefer to roll tea leaves by hand. Drying racks or trays are necessary when gently drying the processed leaves while retaining their flavors and fragrances. A dehumidifier may be helpful in areas that have high humidity levels to keep appropriate drying conditions.

The transformation of shade-grown tea leaves into the fine powder distinctive of matcha, a Japanese green tea, requires using a stone mill or grinder. This machinery is crucial for those who are embarking into the realm of matcha production. By grinding the leaves slowly and deliberately, the stone mill ensures that the matcha retains its delicate flavors and brilliant green color. The very laborious procedure at the heart of matcha preparation is a significant contributor to the distinctive qualities that distinguish this highly regarded tea.

Storage containers are a significant factor to consider to maintain the quality and freshness of your homegrown tea. When tea leaves are stored in airtight containers, preferably made of glass or ceramic, they are shielded from the elements, including air, moisture, and light, all of which have the potential to diminish the flavor and scent of the tea over time. Ensuring that your containers are labeled with the type of tea, the harvest date, and any specific processing notes helps you maintain an organized tea collection. It enables you to appreciate each cup, knowing it comes from a particular place.

In tea gardening, collecting the appropriate instruments is a continual exercise that should be done according to the ever-changing requirements of your garden and your growing expertise in tea production. Beyond the things that can be physically held, the interest and attention mindset is essential. Not only will you cultivate a healthy garden, but you will also cultivate a profound respect for the time-honored custom of producing and enjoying homegrown tea if you observe and care for your tea plants regularly, give them deliberate attention, and have a genuine connection with them. I pray that your tea garden will flourish as you embark on this path and that each cup of tea you brew from your labor of love will bring you closer to the creativity and tranquility tea gardening offers.

CHAPTER II

Planning Your Tea Garden

Choosing the Ideal Location

To ensure the health, vitality, and productivity of your tea plants, selecting the most suitable place for your tea garden is essential. This decision is the first step toward achieving success in your tea garden endeavors. The tea plant, Camellia sinensis, is a flexible species that can adapt to various climates; nonetheless, it is essential to select the appropriate habitat to achieve optimal growth and tea production through the plant. When deciding whether or not a place is suitable for the development of tea, factors such as the amount of sunshine exposure, the quality of the soil, the drainage, and the protection from the elements all play significant roles.

The amount of sunlight tea plants receive is one of the most important aspects determining their overall health and output. For optimal growth, Camellia sinensis should be grown in areas that receive sufficient sunlight, ideally between six and eight hours of direct sunlight each day. When selecting a location for your tea garden, it is essential to consider the patterns of sunlight throughout the day. Particularly advantageous are slopes facing south or areas with uninterrupted east-west exposure, as these provide the most significant amount of sunshine exposure for the most extended period. The growth of tea plants exposed to a sufficient amount of sunshine results in more robust growth, enhanced flavor, and a greater quantity of leaves that are ideal for harvesting.

The cultivation of tea is influenced not only by the amount of sunshine available but also by the microclimate of the selected area. There are specific temperature ranges and humidity levels that tea plants prefer, even though they are adaptive. To pick tea kinds that will flourish in your garden, it is vital to have a solid understanding of the prevalent temperatures and climate patterns in your region. Many tea cultivars, including those belonging to the Assamica subspecies, can thrive in warmer areas. Still, others, such as those belonging to the Sinensis subspecies, are more resistant to colder temperatures. When you plan your tea garden to be in harmony with your area's natural climate, you are laying the groundwork for a highly successful and hardy tea harvest.

When selecting the best place for your tea garden, the soil quality is another essential factor to consider. Camellia sinensis thrives on soil with a pH ranging from slightly acidic to neutral and good drainage. By doing a soil test, you can evaluate the makeup of your soil, including the quantities of nutrients and pH it contains. To promote fertility and drainage, amending the soil with organic matter, such as compost or manure that has been allowed to decompose, is beneficial. In general, sandy or loamy soils are appropriate for tea cultivation, whereas soils that are heavy and clay-based may present difficulties due to inadequate drainage.

There is a clear correlation between drainage and the health of tea plants, making it an essential component of soil quality. The development of root rot and other illnesses can be caused by soil saturated with water, which poses a considerable risk to the health of your tea garden. When picking the place, it is essential to ensure that the chosen spot has adequate drainage to prevent water from building up. It is best to steer clear of low-lying regions prone to flooding, and if it is essential, think about constructing slopes or raised beds to allow efficient water drainage. Not only does soil that drains well protect against root diseases, but it also promotes aeration and the growth of healthy roots.

Tea plants need to be shielded from the components of the environment, particularly in areas that experience severe weather conditions. Even though tea plants can survive minor frosts, they are often vulnerable to extended exposure to frigid temperatures. When growing tea in regions that experience cold winters, it is beneficial to choose a place with natural windbreaks or to build artificial barriers, such as fences or hedgerows, to protect the plants from the cold winds and significant temperature fluctuations. Additionally, during the hot summer months, it is helpful to shelter plants from strong, searing breezes to prevent dehydration and stress on the plants from occurring.

Considering the predominant wind direction and intensity in your region is essential while looking for the perfect spot to plant your tea garden. The prevention of fungal diseases and the promotion of general plant health are both achieved via the use of air circulation that is gentle and well-ventilated. Additionally, windbreaks can serve a dual purpose by providing shade during intense sunlight, reducing excessive evaporation, and assisting in maintaining soil moisture.

Another issue that needs to be evaluated is the selected place's terrain. Even though tea plants can thrive in a wide range of environments, the slope and elevation of your tea garden can impact several aspects, including temperature fluctuations and water drainage. Using sloped topography helps to facilitate natural drainage, which in turn helps reduce waterlogging and promote air circulation. On the other hand, incredibly steep slopes may present difficulties regarding accessibility and contamination control. When you evaluate the terrain, you are able to plan strategically. You can employ contour planting or terracing to accomplish the best possible layout for the tea garden.

In addition to these practically relevant considerations, artistic and cultural aspects also play a role in determining your chosen area. Increasing the visual appeal of your outdoor space can be accomplished by establishing a tea garden that is in harmony with the surrounding scenery and complements the already present vegetation. In addition, if you intend to incorporate items into your tea garden, such as seating places or ornamental features, selecting a location that offers a nice view and is easy to access becomes of the utmost importance.

Several things can influence the microclimates that exist inside your garden. These include the closeness of structures, trees, and bodies of water. It is essential to conduct a comprehensive analysis of these microclimates to discover any potential pockets of warmth or coolness that may affect the growth patterns of your tea varieties. A warmer microclimate can be created in colder places by positioning your tea garden close to a wall or structure that faces south. This provides protection against frost and extends the growth season; it is also beneficial for the tea garden.

Because tea plants require sufficient and continuous watering, you must consider the water source to ensure the success of your tea garden. Although tea plants are usually able to adapt to a variety of water conditions, it is crucial to have a water source that is both clean and reliable to steer clear of contaminants that could have a detrimental effect on the health of the plant. To facilitate frequent and controlled watering, it is essential to ensure that the place you have picked is easily accessible to a water supply, whether it be from a hose, a drip irrigation system, or a natural water source.

Aside from these practical concerns, it is of the utmost importance to ensure that the site of your tea garden matches your gardening objectives and lifestyle. Consider how your tea garden will complement the other plants and components that you have incorporated into your garden design if you choose to incorporate them into an existing landscape. Moreover, the ease with which you care for your tea plants and the regularity with which you do so may be affected by factors such as accessibility and proximity to your living space.

To create a tea garden, one must use a comprehensive approach that incorporates both the aesthetic and practical components of gardening. You may lay the groundwork for a flourishing tea garden by selecting the perfect location. This will not only result in abundant harvests but also provide a tranquil and harmonious environment where tea can be grown. As you embark on your adventure of horticulture, the spot you have chosen will become a haven where the art of producing tea will blend in perfectly with the surrounding area's natural beauty.

Designing Your Tea Sanctuary

Combining the peacefulness of tea culture with the art of gardening, designing a tea sanctuary is an intensely personal and creative activity. Whether you have a little balcony, a modest backyard, or a vast garden, transforming your outdoor space into a refuge for tea cultivation requires careful planning and a good taste for aesthetics. This is true regardless of the size of your outdoor space. Constructing a tea sanctuary is an opportunity to craft a space that symbolizes your love for tea and the natural world. This can be accomplished by selecting the appropriate plants, creating a serene atmosphere, and incorporating functional objects.

When constructing your tea sanctuary, one of the first things you should consider is selecting the appropriate tea plants to your preferences and the area's temperature. Camellia sinensis, the tea plant, comes in various cultivars, each of which contributes a distinct personality to your tea garden. These cultivars offer a wide range of flavors. Your choice of tea plants will determine the atmosphere you want to create, regardless of whether you go for Assam's robustness, Bai Mu Dan's delicacy, or Tie Guan Yin's complexity. When choosing the plants that will serve as the focal point of your tea sanctuary, it is essential to consider the dimensions of your area, the conditions under which they will grow, and the kinds of tea you prefer.

The arrangement of your tea garden is a crucial factor that contributes to the garden's overall design. Thoughtful placement improves tea plants' practicality and aesthetic appeal, regardless of whether you have a tea garden specifically designed for tea or incorporate tea plants into your existing landscape. Create distinct spaces within your garden, such as a planting bed for tea bushes, a seating area for tea ceremonies, and a shady spot for contemplation if you have the space to do so. Paths or stepping stones can direct visitors through the garden, fostering a sense of discovery and encouraging investigation. Pay close attention to the flow of the space and ensure that the various components are in a harmonious balance with one another.

Consider including seating features in your tea sanctuary to create a setting that is both pleasant and conducive to reflection while you sip your organic tea. The setting should be designed to encourage relaxation and a sense of connection with nature, regardless of whether it is a straightforward bench, a set of chairs, or even cushions spread on the ground. An intimate experience can be created by positioning chairs near your tea plants. This will enable you to fully immerse yourself in the sights, smells, and sounds of your garden while partaking in the experience of drinking freshly brewed tea. Your seated area should be surrounded by fragrant plants, such as lavender or mint, whose scents complement the tea leaves. This will enhance the sensory experience and make everything more enjoyable.

Consider incorporating a small table or tea cart into your tea sanctuary in addition to additional chairs. In addition to offering a specific space for teapots, cups, and other accessories, this practical component also functions as a surface ideal for preparing and serving tea. At the same time, a table can be used as a focus point by being ornamented with items that reflect your style. Some examples of such elements include candles, incense, and ornate teaware. The materials and colors of the table you choose should be carefully considered, and you should ensure that they are in harmony with the overall aesthetic of your tea garden.

Your tea sanctuary's visual character and atmosphere are influenced by the materials you choose to employ in its construction. Using natural elements such as wood, stone, and clay can evoke a sense of harmony with the natural world. These materials could be used for various purposes, including seating, paths, or decorative components. Using clay pots or planters can improve the earthy atmosphere of your tea garden while adding wooden benches or stone pavers can lend an air of rustic allure to the property. Incorporate these materials carefully to achieve cohesiveness and unity throughout the entire area.

The tranquility of your tea sanctuary can be enhanced by adding water features, such as a bubbling water basin or a somewhat sizeable fountain. Additionally, the sound of water trickling provides a calming background for your tea rituals, which helps to cultivate a sense of peace and relaxation. A strategic placement of water features should be considered to ensure that they complement the overall design and serve as a visual focal point. A sense of depth and tranquility can be added to your garden by the water's mirrored surface, which can also enhance the meditative aspects of tea cultivation.

When it comes to extending the utilization of your tea sanctuary into the evening hours, lighting is a significant factor to consider. Incorporating aspects of outdoor lighting into your garden will help you create a cozy and welcoming atmosphere, which is ideal for enjoying your garden after the sun has set. Lights that are strung together, lanterns, or garden lights that are strategically placed can be used to highlight pathways, seating spaces, and other essential aspects of your tea garden. You can continue to enjoy your tea sanctuary well into the night if the lighting is soft and diffused. This will enhance the magical essence of the environment.

In addition to the tea bushes themselves, plants contribute to the overall aesthetic and sensory experience of your tea garden when you visit it. If you want to improve the aesthetics and aroma of the area, consider using a combination of fragrant and attractive plants. Not only can lavender, jasmine, and chamomile contribute to the aesthetic attractiveness of a tea vessel, but they also emit lovely odors that perfectly complement the aromas of freshly brewed tea. It is possible to plant herbs such as mint, lemon balm, and basil so that they are easily accessible throughout the process of producing herbal infusions or garnishing your tea. In addition, flowers that bloom during different times of the year ensure that your tea sanctuary is a dynamic and ever-changing landscape.

It can enhance the significance and resonance of your tea sanctuary by using cultural or symbolic things. Think about incorporating aspects representative of the history and customs associated with tea cultures, such as ornamental teapots, bamboo utensils, or ceramic tea cups. Embrace the Japanese tea ceremony by decorating your garden with components reminiscent of the ceremonial, such as a straightforward stone lantern or a stepping-stone pathway. These additions enhance the visual complexity of your tea sanctuary and form a connection between your space and the larger cultural tapestry that is tea.

Creating a tactile and grounding experience in your tea garden can be accomplished through pathways or sections containing loose gravel or mulch. When you walk barefoot on these surfaces, especially if they lead to your seating area or the area where you prepare tea, you add a sensory depth to your experience in the garden. When you walk through your tea sanctuary, the sensation of diverse textures underfoot strengthens your connection with nature and encourages you to take your time and relish each step as you make your way through the space.

Accept the concepts of feng shui or any other design philosophy that resonates with your vision for the tea garden and incorporate them into your creation. In particular, Feng shui emphasizes the flow of energy, also known as "qi," by manipulating components. Consider how the arrangement of tea plants, seats, and ornamental elements corresponds with the concepts of equilibrium, harmony, and positive energy flow. Because of this comprehensive approach, the arrangement of items in your tea sanctuary can be guided, creating a setting that not only satisfies the sense of sight but also nurtures the spirit.

For your tea sanctuary to be thriving, you must strike a balance between its aesthetics and its practicality. Even though aesthetics and design are of the utmost importance, it is important not to forget practical issues such as accessibility, simplicity of maintenance, and suitability for tea growth. It is essential to select plant species that not only add to the aesthetic appeal of your garden but are also well-suited to your area's climate and growing conditions. Ensuring that the walkways and seating spaces are comfortable and easy to navigate is also essential. This will enable you to appreciate and engage with your tea sanctuary completely.

In conclusion, constructing your tea sanctuary is an all-encompassing and gratifying endeavor that combines horticulture, aesthetics, and the artistic expression of the individual. Creating a tea sanctuary provides an opportunity to connect with nature, practice mindfulness, and revel in the simple pleasures of tea culture. This is true regardless of whether you have a green thumb or are just beginning to discover the joys of gardening. Your tea sanctuary should become a refuge of tranquility, a reflection of your love for tea, and a source of inspiration for both the seasoned tea enthusiast and the aspiring tea gardener as you embark on this creative path. It is a place where you can find inspiration.

Soil Preparation and Amendments

The foundation of a thriving tea garden lies beneath the surface – in the soil that cradles the roots of the Camellia sinensis plants. Soil preparation is an essential component that plays a significant role in determining the health, vitality, and flavor profile of the collected leaves to cultivate tea successfully. It is vital to be thoroughly aware of the complexities of soil preparation and the function that amendments play in developing an environment conducive to the growth of tea plants, regardless of whether you are an experienced tea grower or a novice to the world of Camellia sinensis.

The Camellia sinensis plant, used to make tea, does best on soil with a pH range of slightly acidic to neutral and good drainage. Root rot and other illnesses can be caused by soil that retains an excessive amount of water, which poses a considerable risk to the health of tea plants. As a result, ensuring that your tea garden has adequate drainage is the first stage in preparing the soil for it. Incorporating organic matter, such as compost or manure that has been well-rotted, can increase drainage in your garden by improving the soil structure. This is especially helpful if the soil is heavy or clayey. This additive not only helps to prevent waterlogging but also promotes aeration, which enables the roots of the tea plant to breathe and allows them to absorb nutrients more effectively.

Conducting a soil test to determine the makeup of the soil, the levels of nutrients it contains, and its pH is an essential step in preparing the soil for tea farming. Based on the findings of this analysis, you will gain valuable insights into the specific requirements of your soil, which will help you select the proper supplements. Even though tea plants are relatively versatile, they thrive on soils with a pH between 5.5 and 6.5. Should your soil tend to be more alkaline, adding sulfur can assist in lowering the pH, so producing an environment that is more acidic and, hence, more suitable for the cultivation of tea.

Tea plants may flourish without the need for significant amendments in areas with naturally acidic soils, such as those found in certain parts of the United States. Because environmental conditions and other gardening methods can affect the soil's acidity over time, it is still essential to monitor pH levels regularly. The objective is to keep the pH level at a level that is within the appropriate range for Camellia sinensis. This will ensure the plant can absorb nutrients to their full potential and achieve overall health.

When it comes to promoting the growth and development of tea plants, the soil's nutritional content is a significant factor, considering drainage and pH levels. Primary nutrients that tea plants require in variable amounts during their lifecycle include nitrogen, phosphorus, and potassium. Tea plants need these minerals in varying amounts. Incorporating a well-balanced fertilizer containing these vital nutrients lays the groundwork for robust growth and vivid leaves. Not only can organic fertilizers, such as compost or manure that has been allowed to decompose over time, provide the soil with the nutrients it needs, but they also add to the soil's overall health by encouraging the activity of beneficial microorganisms.

One of the most important things to do is to understand tea plants' nitrogen requirements. Nitrogen is an essential component in the development of leaves and the overall vitality of the plant. As a general rule, tea plants favor moderate quantities of nitrogen; nevertheless, excessive nitrogen can result in quick and luxuriant growth, albeit at the price of flavor. To achieve optimal equilibrium, it is essential to utilize organic sources of nitrogen, such as fish emulsion or composted poultry manure, which offer a supply that is both slow- release and sustainable.

For tea plants to establish their roots and flower, phosphorus is essential. The presence of sufficient amounts of phosphorus assists in developing robust root systems, ensuring that the plant can effectively absorb water and nutrients. Bone meal is a popular organic amendment that is abundant in phosphorus. It encourages the formation of healthy roots without the adverse effects of an excessive amount of nitrogen.

Regarding general plant health and resistance to disease, potassium, the third primary nutrient, is absolutely necessary. Potassium is essential for the development of resilient tea plants because it governs a variety of physiological activities, including the utilization of water and the process of photosynthesis. Greensand, a naturally occurring mineral source of potassium, can be integrated into the soil to offer a supply of this essential nutrient that would be released gradually.

When it comes to tea gardens, compost, frequently referred to as "black gold" in the gardening community, is an adaptable and beneficial amendment. The addition of compost not only improves the structure and fertility of the soil but also introduces a wide variety of microorganisms that are helpful to the soil. These bacteria contribute to the soil's health by enhancing water retention, increasing the cycling of nutrients, and inhibiting the growth of pathogens damaging to the soil. The organic matter included within compost also provides tea plants with a supply of nutrients that are released gradually over a lengthy period.

Compost can be integrated into the soil during the initial planting phase or applied as a top dressing during the growth season. Both of these applications are considered to be amendments. It functions as a natural fertilizer, delivering a balanced assortment of nutrients, such as nitrogen, phosphorus, and potassium, so plants can flourish. Applying compost consistently helps to build a soil structure that is rich and loamy, which facilitates the growth of tea plants in an environment that is conducive to their success.

The heavy metals and other toxins that are present in the soil can have a particularly negative impact on tea plants. To guarantee the safety of your tea leaves, it is crucial to conduct soil testing to identify any potential toxins. This is especially important if you are gardening in urban or industrial surroundings. It is possible for heavy metals like lead and cadmium to accumulate in tea leaves, which, if drunk, could constitute a threat to one's health. Remediation steps may be required if contamination is found. Additionally, it may be prudent to investigate alternative planting places or the utilization of raised beds filled with soil that is not polluted.

In tea gardening, mulching is an excellent strategy that not only helps preserve the soil's moisture content but also adds to the management of weeds and the soil's overall health. Applying a layer of organic mulch, which may consist of straw, wood chips, or shredded leaves, makes it possible to control the temperature of the soil, stop the loss of moisture, and inhibit the growth of weeds. Not only does mulch gradually decompose, but it also contributes organic matter to the soil and encourages the activity of microorganisms. On the other hand, it is crucial to maintain a balance while applying mulch. It is essential to ensure that the mulch does not gather too close to the base of the tea plants, as this might produce an environment conducive to the growth of diseases and pests.

The soil preparation involves more than just the planting phase at the beginning of your tea garden; it continues throughout its existence. Consistently monitoring the conditions of the soil, the levels of nutrients, and the pH ensures that you can make adjustments promptly to support the ever-changing requirements of tea plants. It is possible to further improve soil fertility by incorporating cover crops in between tea rows during the dormant season. This can be accomplished by fixing nitrogen, avoiding erosion, and stimulating microbial activity.

When it comes to successful tea gardening, the preparation of the soil and the addition of nutrients are essential components that have a significant impact on the health, flavor, and The total vitality of plants belonging to the Camellia sinensis species. A number of factors contribute to the construction of an environment appropriate to the cultivation of tea with care and accuracy. These factors include completing soil testing, understanding the specific requirements that tea plants have, and introducing organic amendments. Your efforts to prepare the soil will provide the groundwork for an abundant harvest and a flourishing tea sanctuary as you embark on the path of tea farming.

CHAPTER III

Getting Started with Seeds and Seedlings

Overview of Tea Plant Propagation

The propagation of tea plants, Camellia sinensis, is a nuanced and essential aspect of tea cultivation that determines the success and sustainability of a tea garden. The techniques used to propagate tea plants are extremely important since they are responsible for establishing new plants, preserving genetic features, and guaranteeing the uninterrupted production of tea. The various methods of propagation, ranging from seeds to cuttings, each have their own set of advantages, disadvantages, and implications for the development and quality of the produced tea plants.

It is possible to propagate tea plants using seeds, one of the primary methods. Seeds are a natural and cost-effective reproduction method, yet they come with problems that require patience and careful attention. Seeds are a natural way of reproduction. In most cases, tea seeds are discovered within the fruits, also known as "pods," of mature tea plants. Seeds that have been harvested must go through a process known as stratification, which involves exposing them to settings that are cold and wet for a period of time to break their dormancy. At the same time that it prepares the seeds for germination, this simulates the natural cycle of the seasons.

The germination process for tea seeds can take anything from a few weeks to many months, depending on the soil that has been adequately prepared. Several elements, including temperature, humidity, and the particular variety of tea, can affect the timing of the germination process. Considering how fragile they are in their early stages, the seedlings produced require careful attention. The seedlings will eventually mature into young tea plants as they grow; however, it may take several years for them to reach maturity and become productive enough to meet harvesting requirements.

Although cultivating tea plants from seeds offers a link to the plant's natural life cycle, it also takes a significant investment of time and patience on the grower's part. Furthermore, the genetic diversity inherent in seeds might result in variances in features among the plants produced as a natural consequence. Beginning with seeds can be a gratifying and informative experience for individuals who appreciate the process of cultivating tea plants from their earliest stages when they are still young.

Another method extensively used for reproducing tea plants is cutting propagation, which offers a more controlled and faster approach than seed propagation. Cutting propagation is also widely employed. Cuttings, which are little parts of mature tea plant stems, and stimulating them to develop roots is the technique involved in this process. Growers can mimic the features of a well-established tea plant using this procedure, which guarantees stability in both the flavor profiles and the development patterns of the tea plant throughout its life.

During the dormant season, when the plants are less actively growing, the cuttings are often obtained from mature tea plants that are no longer susceptible to disease. Following the selection of the stems, often known as "cuttings," rooting hormones are administered to the stems to encourage the growth of roots. After the cuttings have been treated, they are then planted in a rooting media that is appropriate for them, such as a mixture of peat moss and perlite. The process of rooting is made more accessible by providing the right conditions, which include maintaining a comfortable temperature and humidity level.

While cutting propagation has several benefits, including the preservation of genetic features and a reduction in the time needed to reach maturity, it also necessitates a particular set of abilities and careful attention to detail. For a cutting to successfully root, a number of elements must be considered, including the age of the cutting, the season, and the overall health of the parent plant. Additionally, before being transplanted into the tea garden, the growing plants could need to be carefully acclimatized to the circumstances that are found outside.

In the past few years, tissue culture has evolved as a contemporary and effective method of growing tea plants worldwide. Developing plant cells in a laboratory environment is known as tissue culture. This technique enables the mass production of plants that are genetically similar to one another. This technique allows for fine control over the propagation process, guaranteeing that all traits and attributes are consistent. Using tissue culture is especially beneficial for large-scale tea plantations and nurseries looking to create a constant supply of plants swiftly.

When beginning the tissue culture process, the first step is to collect plant tissues, typically taken from early shoots or leaves. Following this, the tissues are cultivated in a medium rich in nutrients while maintaining sterile conditions. Plantlets are carefully cultivated until they reach a stage where they can acclimate to the external environment and shift to conventional soil-based cultivation. This process continues until the plantlets reach the developmental stage.

Even though tissue culture makes the propagation process more efficient and results in genetically similar plants with desirable characteristics, it necessitates the use of specialized equipment, experience, and facilities. There are potential obstacles for smaller-scale tea growers, such as the initial investment and the need for more technical know-how. However, as technology continues to progress and become more readily available, tissue culture shows promise to improve the effectiveness and uniformity of tea plant multiplication across various production scales.

The timing of planting or transplanting tea plants is an important aspect that must be taken into account regardless of the selected method of propagation. When it comes to planting, the dormant season, which usually occurs in late autumn or early spring, is frequently favored since it allows the plants to establish their root systems before the beginning of the vigorous growth phase. Additionally, the dormant phase coincides with conditions ideal for root formation, increasing the likelihood of successful establishment.

Consideration should also be given to the distance between tea plants during propagation and planting. To provide optimal sun exposure, air circulation, and ease of care, adequate spacing is necessary. The particular spacing needs may change depending on the type of tea, the area's environment, and the planned pruning procedures. Maintaining an appropriate distance between plants helps to ensure healthy growth, lowers the likelihood of illnesses, and makes harvesting more effective.

There is a strong correlation between the quality of the soil in which tea plants are planted and the success of propagating and establishing tea plants. A foundation that is appropriate for the cultivation of tea is soil with a pH that ranges from slightly acidic to neutral and good drainage. Fertility and overall soil health are improved by adding soil amendments, such as compost or manure, that have been allowed to decompose. It is vital to carry out a comprehensive investigation of the soil in the position that has been selected to identify any shortages or imbalances that may affect the growth of tea plants.

To summarize, the process of propagating tea plants is an essential phase in the process of building and sustaining a tea garden space. Each technique, whether through tissue culture, cuttings, or seeds, comes with its own set of benefits and factors to consider. Not only does the propagation process determine the genetic makeup of the tea plants, but it also impacts the effectiveness of tea production and the overall performance of the garden. The skill of tea gardening is becoming increasingly popular among tea enthusiasts and cultivators.

When it comes to the journey that begins with planting seeds or cuttings and ends with harvesting magnificent leaves for brewing, the careful selection of tea plants and the intentional propagation of those plants become crucial components.

Starting from Seeds

Beginning the process of growing tea from its seeds is an adventure that allows fans to engage with the natural life cycle of the Camellia sinensis plant, which is traditionally used to produce tea. Growing tea from seeds is a one-of-a-kind and satisfying experience, even though it needs patience and a more extended gestation period in comparison to other techniques of propagation. To complete the process, the tiny seeds must be cultivated through the stages of germination, seedling development, and, finally, the maturation of robust tea plants that are ready to be harvested. This method not only enables growers to gain a more profound comprehension of the plant's life cycle but also allows them to see the development of their tea garden from its most preliminary stages.

Tea seeds, contained within the pods of mature tea plants, can bring forth new life and ensure that the tea tradition will continue beyond this generation. A deliberate effort that requires timing, care, and respect for the cyclical nature of tea cultivation, harvesting these seeds is a process that requires careful attention. After being collected, the seeds go through a process that is referred to as stratification. During this process, the seeds are exposed to cold and moist temperatures, which are meant to simulate the natural seasonal changes that cause the seeds to break their dormancy.

The process of stratification is an essential step in the process of getting the seeds ready for germination. In addition to indicating that the seeds have emerged from their state of dormancy, it also causes biochemical changes within the seeds, preparing them to transform into sprouting seedlings. A more profound connection with the essence of tea growing can be fostered through this natural, hands-on technique, which allows tea fans to participate in the intricate dance between the plant and its surroundings.

As soon as the stratification process is complete, the tea seeds are carefully planted in soil that has been thoroughly prepared. This marks the beginning of the germination period. Patience is a virtue during this time because the amount of time it takes for tea seeds to germinate can vary depending on several factors, including temperature, humidity, and the particular type of tea. When fragile shoots sprout from the earth, it is a moment of anticipation and celebration because it marks the beginning of the trip that the tea plant will take from seed to maturity during its lifetime.

As the seedlings emerge, they must be carefully tended to to guarantee they will develop healthily. A delicate balance must be maintained between sunlight, water, and protection from environmental stresses for tea plants as they are in their early stages of development. Each little shot represents the promise of future growth and the possibility of a flourishing tea garden. The frail seedlings begin to sprout leaves, and each tiny shoot defines that promise.

During the early stages of seedling development, the plant's growth habits, leaf traits, and overall vitality are all influenced by the earliest phases, which provide the framework for the later stages of the plant's development. To ensure that these young tea plants are adequately cared for, it is necessary to provide them with the ideal circumstances for photosynthesis, the establishment of roots, and the development of a sturdy structure. The greenhouse or other indoor environment is a safe refuge for these young tea plants, protecting them from the unpredictable weather and other dangers from the outside world.

During their development, the tea plants move from the hospitable limits of indoor rooms to the atmosphere of the outdoors. The seedlings can adjust to the changes in temperature, humidity, and sunlight during the acclimatization phase, which becomes a critical phase. By undergoing this slow shift, the young plants are prepared for life in the open air, where they will eventually take root and establish themselves as essential components of the tea garden.

A critical decision must be made regarding the timing of the transplanting of tea seedlings into the garden. This decision must strike a balance between the preparedness of the plants and the conditions of the external environment. When it comes to transplanting, the dormant season, which often occurs in late autumn or early spring, is generally preferred because it coincides with the time of year when plants are less actively growing. By strategically scheduling their planting, the tea plants can develop their root systems before the beginning of their robust growth. This increases the likelihood that they will survive and successfully integrate into the garden.

While transplanting tea plants, it is essential to consider the spacing between each plant, as this affects the general health and production of the garden. To provide optimal sun exposure, air circulation, and ease of care, adequate spacing is essential. The particular spacing requirements may change depending on the type of tea, the climate of the area, and the pruning procedures intended to be used. It is essential to ensure that each tea plant gets the space it requires to flourish and contribute to the overall harmony of the tea garden. This can be accomplished by careful planning and layout.

When successfully transitioning tea plants from seedlings to garden residents, soil preparation is an essential component that must be achieved. A foundation that is appropriate for the cultivation of tea is soil with a pH that ranges from slightly acidic to neutral and good drainage. Amendments to the soil, such as compost or manure that has been allowed to decompose, improve the fertility of the soil and the overall health of the soil, so producing an environment that is conducive to the growth of tea plants. It is essential to carry out a comprehensive investigation of the soil in the selected area to identify any shortages or imbalances that may affect the growth of tea plants.

Getting from the seed to the garden is a process that requires constant attention and care during the entire journey. The tea gardener is responsible for performing everyday chores such as monitoring the health of the tea plants, supplying their plants with continuous watering, and safeguarding them from illnesses and pests. The tea garden should be observed regularly so that any potential problems may be identified at an early stage. This will enable timely interventions, ensuring the tea garden's continuous health.

The development of tea plants from seeds is a gradual unfolding of nature's design, and each stage of the process contributes to the distinctive personality of the tea produced. Investing time and effort pays off in a garden full of blooming tea plants, even though it may take several years to achieve maturity and yield appropriate leaves for harvesting. The act of beginning from seeds not only results in a rich harvest but also instills a sense of accomplishment and a profound connection to the cycles of life that occur in the tea garden.

It is a tradition that has been passed down from generation to generation and celebrates the natural rhythms of the plant. Tea enthusiasts who cultivate tea from seeds are participating in this tradition. When it comes to good tea cultivation, patience and perseverance are essential qualities, and the garden serves as a living monument to these qualities. The journey from seed to cup becomes a narrative woven with care, curiosity, and a profound appreciation for the beauty of tea growing. This narrative begins with the initial germination of seeds and continues until the leaves appear lively and are ready to be harvested.

Caring for Young Tea Seedlings

As tea enthusiasts embark on cultivating their tea gardens, the care and attention given to young tea seedlings play a pivotal role in establishing the foundation for a thriving and productive garden. It is necessary to thoroughly comprehend the requirements and vulnerabilities of young tea plants throughout each phase, beginning with the delicate emergence of seedlings and ending with their eventual transplantation into the outdoor environment. It is necessary to balance several parameters carefully to care for these young tea family members properly. These factors include exposure to light, watering, protection from environmental stressors, and the progressive shift from indoor to outdoor growth environments. This section goes into the art of caring for young tea seedlings, examining the complexities of their early phases and providing insights into building an environment conducive to robust growth and future harvests.

Germination is the first step in caring for new tea seedlings, which is the first phase of the procedure. After being subjected to stratification to break dormancy, the seeds are then planted in soil that has been thoroughly prepared. The growers eagerly await the appearance of small shoots, indicating the beginning of the seedlings' journey. Patience becomes a virtue during this time. It is essential to ensure that the circumstances for germination are kept at their ideal level at this critical stage. Successful germination is achieved when the young tea plants have sufficient warmth, moisture, and protection from direct sunshine. This creates the conditions for young tea plants to unfold their initial leaves.

For the seeds to germinate, they need to be placed in a stimulating indoor environment. This is typically made possible by the regulated circumstances in a greenhouse or other indoor growing facility. The delicate seedlings are protected from sudden shifts in temperature, severe weather, and potential pests if placed in these regions, providing a protected environment for the early phases of their development. Natural sunshine can be supplemented by grow lights, which ensures that seedlings receive the appropriate quantity and quality of light for photosynthesis and overall development. Grow lights can be used to augment natural sunlight.

Light exposure is essential to care for new tea seedlings properly. Even while tea plants do best when exposed to bright, indirect light, any amount of light that is either too much or too little might hurt their growth. Monitoring the intensity and duration of sunshine or artificial light sources is required to achieve a satisfactory level of light exposure. When there is not enough light, seedlings can become lean and extended, but when there is too much light, the seedlings might become scorched or stressed. It is possible to create an atmosphere similar to the dotted sunshine conditions that young tea plants love by adjusting the positioning of grow lights or giving partial shading.

Precision and consistency are essential criteria when it comes to watering young tea seedlings. Inadequate watering offers a considerable concern, as it might result in soil saturated with water and possibly root rot. On the other hand, submerging plants in water can inhibit their growth and put their health at risk. Keeping the soil continually moist without allowing it to become saturated is an integral part of striking the appropriate balance. It is possible to reduce the amount of water that accumulates by using soil that drains appropriately and containers with drainage holes. When watering, it is essential to be gentle and to avoid coming into close touch with the fragile leaves to avoid causing any harm or sickness.

The seedlings go through the crucial stage of developing their first set of genuine leaves as they continue to build on their development path. There is a distinction between these leaves and the original cotyledons, which are a component of the embryonic structure of the seed. When genuine leaves appear on a plant, this marks the beginning of photosynthesis, which is how plants convert sunlight into energy. During this stage, it is possible to use a gentle and well-balanced fertilizer to supply the necessary nutrients to develop healthy leaves. Some examples of organic fertilizers include compost tea that has been diluted or a mild liquid fertilizer. These types of fertilizers provide a steady and gradual delivery of nutrients.

Protecting against environmental stresses is a continuing aspect that must be considered in maintaining young tea seedlings. There is a potential for sensitive plants to be affected by draughts, unexpected temperature changes, and fluctuations in humidity. It is beneficial to their strong growth and resilience to protect them from these stressors, particularly in the early phases of development. In addition to this, it is essential to conduct routine inspections to look for indications of diseases or pests. Aphids, spider mites, and fungal infections are some of the most common unwanted organisms that can damage tea seedlings. Through natural cures or the introduction of beneficial predators, such as ladybugs, it is possible to maintain an environment that is both healthy and resistant to pests.

When it comes to maintaining young tea seedlings, one of the most important moments is moving from indoor to outdoor environments. The plants are gradually exposed to the environment's conditions through acclimatization, which prepares them for the eventual relocation to the garden. This phase usually occurs during the dormant season, corresponding to either the end of fall or the beginning of spring. When seedlings are exposed to the elements of the outdoors in a controlled manner, they can adjust to the natural light, temperature fluctuations, and mild winds that are present in the open air. It is possible to reduce the stress associated with transplantation through acclimatization, making the transfer more seamless and increasing the possibility of successful establishment in the garden.

Before planting the young tea seedlings in the garden, carefully considering the planting distance between each plant is essential. To provide optimal sun exposure, air circulation, and ease of care, adequate spacing is necessary. The particular spacing requirements may change depending on the type of tea, the climate of the area, and the pruning procedures intended to be used. Providing sufficient space for each plant to flourish adds to the development of healthy plants, lowers the danger of suffering from diseases, and makes it easier to harvest plants in the future.

When it comes to caring for new tea seedlings throughout the transplantation process, soil preparation is an essential action to take. A foundation appropriate for tea cultivation is soil with a pH that ranges from slightly acidic to neutral and has good drainage. Fertility and overall soil health are improved by adding soil amendments, such as compost or manure, that have been allowed to decompose. It is necessary to conduct a comprehensive investigation of the soil in the selected area to identify any shortages or imbalances that may affect the growth of tea plants. When the soil is prepared, the young seedlings are placed in an environment favorable to their continuous development and eventual maturation.

After the young tea seedlings have been transplanted into the garden, their care continues, emphasizing performing regular maintenance and making observations. They continue to require regular watering, protection from pests, and monitoring for signs of stress or nutrient deficits as essential components of their care. Mulching the area around the plants retains soil moisture, prevents the growth of weeds, and controls the temperature of the soil. It may be essential to provide the young plants with adequate support, such as stakes or ties, to shield them from the damaging effects of strong winds or heavy rain. This will also provide them more stability throughout their initial period in the garden.

As the immature tea seedlings develop into mature plants, the function of the caretaker gradually shifts from that of a nurturer to that of a curator. The general health and production of the tea plants can be improved by pruning and shaping them. During pruning, branching is encouraged, growth is regulated, and the quality of the harvested leaves is improved. It is possible for the timing and method of pruning to change depending on the type of tea plant and the shape that is wanted for the plant. The continuing care and maintenance techniques are guided by regular assessments of the plant's overall health, vigor, and leaf quality.

The process of caring for young tea seedlings is a complex and ongoing endeavor that requires a combination of scientific understanding and gardening methods that are thoughtful and attentive. To cultivate an atmosphere where new tea plants can flourish, each stage of the process, beginning with the delicate germination phase and ending with transplanting the plants into the garden, calls for a thoughtful approach. They start on a trip that connects them with the cycles of nature, the artistry of cultivation, and the promise of future harvests. As caretakers of these young tea family members, enthusiasts experience a journey that connects them with these elements. The expectation of a flourishing tea garden resides in the meticulous care of young tea seedlings. The leaves sprout from these delicate plants will one day grace the teapot, delivering the essence of a journey that began with a tiny seed. This anticipation is achieved via the careful cultivating of young tea seedlings.

CHAPTER IV

Nurturing Your Tea Plants

Watering and Irrigation Techniques

In the intricate dance of tea cultivation, the role of water cannot be overstated. It is essential for the health of tea plants, their growth, and the quality of the tea that is produced that they receive adequate hydration at every stage of their development, from the tender seedling stage to the mature bushes that are heavy with leaves. One of the most critical aspects of practical tea gardening is having a solid understanding of the fundamentals of watering and implementing the necessary irrigation procedures. The art and science of watering tea plants are investigated in this section. Topics covered include the factors that determine water needs, the significance of soil moisture management, and the numerous irrigation methods tailored to meet the specific requirements of the Camellia sinensis plant.

The water requirements of tea plants change throughout their lifecycle, and the success of a tea garden is directly proportional to the level of care provided at each stage of the plant's development. Young tea seedlings, which are still in the delicate phase of their development, require a watering routine that is both balanced and consistent. Both overwatering and underwatering can cause the soil to become saturated, leading to root rot and other diseases. On the other hand, underwatering can impede growth and put the health of the seedlings at risk. Achieving the ideal equilibrium requires maintaining a steady moisture level in the soil without completely saturating it. To do this, one must take a careful approach, keeping a close eye on the particular requirements of the tea seedlings as they are housed in a safe indoor setting.

Watering tea plants becomes more complicated as they develop from seedlings to large bushes. The plant's capacity to effectively take in water and nutrients is impacted by constructing a robust root system during the early stages of the plant's development or growth. As a result, the control of soil moisture becomes of the utmost importance, and the implementation of watering practices that encourage the establishment of deep roots is vital. Providing tea plants with deep watering helps to foster the growth of a robust and comprehensive root network, which in turn enables the plants to endure periods of drought and have access to water from more profound levels of the soil.

There is a significant relationship between the type of

soil in which tea plants are grown and the amount of water required for their growth. It is optimal for tea growing to have soil that drains well and a pH ranging from slightly acidic to neutral. When it comes to drainage, heavy or clayey soils can be a problem, resulting in soggy situations. On the other hand, sandy soils may drain too rapidly, which requires more regular watering. To provide appropriate care for tea plants, it is essential to do routine soil moisture monitoring and make adjustments to the watering schedule based on the type of soil.

Supplemental irrigation becomes an essential

component of tea planting when there is a lack of constant rainfall or dry periods. Various irrigation techniques are tailored to meet the particular requirements of tea plants, ensuring that water is effectively delivered to the root zone. A technique that is frequently utilized in tea plantations is known as drip irrigation. This technique involves the gradual and targeted flow of water directly to each plant's root. It is possible to exercise exact control over the amount of water provided to individual plants, which helps limit the danger of foliar diseases and minimize the amount of water wasted.

Another technique frequently used in tea cultivation is sprinkler irrigation, which is particularly prevalent in larger estates. It is possible to achieve a consistent water distribution across the tea bushes by employing this method, which entails water administration in droplets or tiny spray. Even though sprinkler systems are effective at covering vast areas, careful management is required to prevent water loss due to evaporation and decrease the tea leaves' soaking, which might raise the risk of fungal diseases.

An irrigation technique known as furrow or basin irrigation is a time-honored technique that involves the formation of channels or basins around the base of tea plants to direct the flow of water. By utilizing this technique, it is possible to perform regulated irrigation, which allows water to penetrate the root zone gradually. However, basin irrigation is beneficial in more extensive plantations because it will enable water to be concentrated at the foot of each bush. Furrow irrigation suits tiny tea gardens, while basin irrigation is particularly successful in more extensive plantations.

When it comes to tea planting, the time of watering is an essential aspect. Because temperatures and evaporation rates are lower at these times, it is often advised that watering be done in the early morning or late afternoon. It is not recommended to water plants in the evening because the prolonged presence of moisture on the leaves throughout the night can generate conditions conducive to developing fungal diseases. To guarantee that tea plants receive the hydration they require for maximum growth and leaf development, it is essential to water them consistently throughout the growing season, making modifications based on the weather conditions and the soil moisture levels experienced.

Mulching is a complementary method that improves the soil's ability to retain water, reduces the growth of weeds, and maintains a consistent temperature in the soil. Applying a layer of organic mulch around the base of tea plants, such as straw, wood chips, or shredded leaves, helps conserve soil moisture by limiting the amount of water that evaporates into the atmosphere. A further contribution that mulching makes to the soil's overall health is that it encourages the activity of microorganisms and creates a protective barrier that insulates the root zone from temperature fluctuations.

One of the factors that plays a role in determining the overall health of tea plants is the quality of the water used for watering. In a perfect world, the water would be devoid of any impurities, excessive salts, or minerals that could affect the structure of the soil and the nutrient balance. It is common practice to favor rainwater due to its high purity level; nevertheless, if you are reliant on other water sources, conducting periodic soil testing can assist in determining the effect that irrigation water has on the tea garden. It is possible that adjustments, such as leaching to remove accumulated salts, will be required to keep the soil conditions at their optimal level.

Tea plants are susceptible to the quality of the water they are grown in, and the minerals present in the water used for irrigation can affect the flavor profile of the harvested leaves. The tea may have flavors that are not desirable if it has high concentrations of certain minerals, such as fluoride or manganese. To guarantee that the irrigation water supports the cultivation process, it is required to monitor the water quality and, if necessary, perform filter or treatment methods.

When it comes to the art and science of tea growing, watering and irrigation techniques are essential and critical components. In the process of watering, each step adds to the collected tea's overall health, growth, and quality. This includes carefully caring for immature seedlings and managing water resources in more giant farms. It is possible to cultivate an environment in which the Camellia sinensis plant may flourish and produce leaves worthy of the teapot by carefully balancing the amount of moisture in the air, selecting the appropriate watering techniques, and considering the many environmental conditions. It is a tradition that recognizes the essence of cultivation, the interconnection of elements, and the promise of a harvest that reflects careful water management in the art of tea growing. Tea lovers who embrace the complexities of watering their tea garden are participating in this tradition.

Proper Feeding and Fertilization

The job of correct feeding and fertilization takes center stage in the complicated choreography of tea cultivation. There is a strong connection between the nutrient content of the tea plants' soil and the health, vitality, and flavor profile of the tea plants themselves. With the responsibility of becoming stewards of a tea garden, specialists are required to traverse the art and science of feeding tea plants. They must strike a delicate balance that allows the plants to continue growing while improving the collected leaves' quality. This section examines the complex world of correct feeding and fertilization in tea gardening. It looks at the nutritional requirements of the Camellia sinensis plant, the significance of maintaining healthy soil, and the numerous fertilization tactics that contribute to the growth of a flourishing tea garden.

Camellia sinensis, the plant from which tea leaves are collected, is a discriminating organism regarding the nutritional requirements it must fulfill. Even though it is versatile and can thrive in a wide range of climates and soil types, it is essential to be thoroughly aware of its specific requirements to cultivate it successfully. The primary nutrients that tea plants require in variable amounts during their lifecycle are nitrogen, phosphorus, and potassium. Tea plants need these minerals in varying amounts. When it comes to the development of leaves, the formation of roots, and the overall vitality of the plant, these critical substances play crucial roles.

Nitrogen is an essential component of chlorophyll, responsible for the beautiful green color of tea leaves. Nitrogen is also necessary for the vigorous growth of vegetative tissue. The development of amino acids, the fundamental components of proteins, is influenced by the presence of sufficient nitrogen levels, which in turn affects the flavor and quality of the harvested tea. The use of an excessive amount of nitrogen, on the other hand, might result in quick and lush growth at the price of flavor. This delicate balance must be maintained. Composted poultry manure and fish emulsion are two examples of organic sources of nitrogen that offer a slow-release and sustainable supply of nitrogen, thus reducing the risk of over-fertilization.

The development of roots, flowering, and the overall movement of energy throughout the plant depend on phosphorus. When establishing roots is the primary focus during the early stages of a tea plant's life, paying attention to this time is essential. Bone meal and other organic compounds high in phosphorus contribute to developing healthy roots and guarantee that the plant can effectively absorb water and nutrients.

The health of tea plants' health depends on various factors, including potassium, which is the third essential nutrient. It is responsible for regulating multiple physiological activities, including the intake of water, the activation of enzymes, and photosynthesis. The plant's resistance to diseases and other environmental stressors is increased when the plant has adequate levels of potassium. Additionally, greensand, a naturally occurring mineral source of potassium, can be integrated into the soil to deliver this vital nutrient in a more gradual manner.

Nitrogen, phosphorus, and potassium are examples of macronutrients considered necessary for tea plants. However, a wide variety of micronutrients also contribute to tea plants' overall health and well-being. Micronutrients such as iron, manganese, zinc, copper, and boron are among those involved in specialized functions in activating enzymes, photosynthesis, and other biochemical activities. The results of soil tests can assist in determining whether or not there are any deficits in micronutrients. This enables growers to provide targeted amendments to meet specific requirements.

Understanding the specific nutrient requirements of Camellia sinensis and the soil's properties is the cornerstone of adequate feeding and fertilization in tea gardening. This knowledge is necessary for proper feeding and fertilization to be possible. As a result of doing a comprehensive soil analysis, producers can gain insights into the composition of the soil, the quantities of nutrients present, and the pH of the soil, which enables them to make informed decisions regarding fertilization tactics. The utilization of soil testing as a diagnostic technique allows the identification of any imbalances or inadequacies that may impede the growth of tea plants to their full potential.

The term "black gold" is commonly used in the gardening community to describe compost, a flexible and invaluable amendment that plays a vital role in fertilization and feeding plants. The addition of compost not only improves the structure and fertility of the soil but also introduces a wide variety of microorganisms that are helpful to the soil. These bacteria contribute to the soil's health by enhancing water retention, increasing the cycling of nutrients, and inhibiting the growth of pathogens damaging to the soil. The organic matter included within compost also provides tea plants with a supply of nutrients that are released gradually over a lengthy period.

The utilization of compost is by the principles of organic and sustainable agriculture, which helps to create an all-encompassing approach to soil health. There is a correlation between the consistent addition of compost and the formation of a rich, loamy soil structure, creating an environment where tea plants can flourish. The presence of this organic matter contributes to the progressive release of nitrogen, phosphorous, and potassium over time, acting as a reservoir for these nutrients.

Organic fertilizers derived from natural sources, in addition to compost, play an essential part in feeding and fertilizing plants correctly. Tea plants can receive vital nutrients from various organic sources, including fish emulsion, seaweed extracts, and manure that can decompose adequately. In addition to contributing to the fertility of the soil, these organic fertilizers raise the level of microbial activity in the rhizosphere. This results in establishing a mutually beneficial relationship between the tea plant and the soil's ecosystem.

When it comes to tea gardening, mulching is an efficient strategy that works with the successful application of fertilizer and feeding. For several reasons, it is beneficial to spread a layer of organic mulch, such as straw, wood chips, or shredded fallen leaves. Mulch is beneficial to the soil because it acts as a temperature regulator, stops the loss of moisture, inhibits the growth of weeds, and contributes to the soil's overall health. The decomposition of the mulch results in the addition of organic matter to the soil, further enhancing the soil's fertility.

It is also possible for inorganic or synthetic fertilizers to play a part in feeding and fertilizing plants correctly, particularly when specific nutritional imbalances require repair. On the other hand, their utilization necessitates careful study and strict adherence to the indicated application rates. The use of synthetic fertilizers in excessive amounts can result in nutritional imbalances, the degradation of soil, and pollution of the environment. The tea garden's long-term viability can be ensured by using a systematic and prudent approach to fertilizing, which considers both organic and inorganic sources of fertilizer materials.

The time and the frequency of fertilization are essential components of a feeding strategy carried out effectively. To establish a robust root system and promote vegetative development, young tea plants benefit from a mild and consistent supply of nutrients when they are in their early stages of growth. It is possible to adjust the fertilization schedule as the tea plants age, taking into account their growth patterns, the requirements of the season, and the findings of soil tests. The use of many fertilizer applications during the growth season, as opposed to a single hefty dose, helps provide a more regulated release of nutrients and eliminates the possibility of over-fertilization.

In conjunction with soil testing, analysis of the leaves is a beneficial method for determining the nutrient status of tea plants. Keeping an eye on the concentration of nutrients in the collected,This information gives growers insights into the effectiveness of the fertilization program and assists them in making adjustments based on accurate information. Early clues can trigger a deliberate evaluation of the feeding regimen. Some examples of these early indicators include yellowing leaves or leaf tip burn, which are symptoms of nutritional deficits or excesses.

In conclusion, properly feeding and fertilizing tea plants are the foundation of practical tea gardening. These factors have an impact on the health of the tea garden, as well as its flavor and environmental sustainability. Enthusiasts start on a journey beyond cultivation; it becomes a subtle dance with nature as they become aware of the nutritional requirements of Camellia sinensis, the complexities of maintaining healthy soil, and the diverse array of fertilization options. Tea plants absorb the nutrients from the soil and change them into leaves ready to be harvested; the artistry of proper feeding and fertilization unfolds, leaving an indelible mark on the tea's terroir. Not only do tea fans maintain a garden through the careful maintenance of the soil and the attentive application of nutrients, but they also foster a tradition that has been passed down from generation to generation. This tradition celebrates the delicate balance between the plant, the soil, and the essence of tea.

Pest Control and Disease Management

When those passionate about tea begin establishing their own tea garden, the delicate dance with nature becomes the focal point of the spectacle. There is a hazard of pests and illnesses lurking amid the verdant foliage of tea plants, which poses problems to the health of the garden and its output. A careful and holistic strategy that strikes a balance between the need to safeguard the tea plants and the goal of maintaining sustainable and environmentally friendly techniques is required to cultivate tea successfully. During this time, pest control and disease management have become critical components of effective tea cultivation. This section looks into the pest control and disease management domain in tea gardening. It examines the common enemies that tea plants have to contend with, the fundamentals of integrated pest management, and the tactics used to protect the essence of tea.

The tea plants, which are members of the Camellia, are vulnerable to a wide variety of pests that can risk the garden's health and yield. Tea plants are susceptible to various pests, including aphids, mites, scale insects, and caterpillars, among its most common enemies. If these pests are not controlled, they can inflict damage to the plant by feeding on the leaves, causing disruptions in the plant's growth and perhaps transferring diseases. Therefore, monitoring and proactive actions are required to preserve a healthy balance between tea plants and the natural predators that they face.

Integrated pest management (IPM), which promotes a comprehensive and environmentally responsible approach to pest control, is becoming increasingly prevalent in the growing tea. IPM acknowledges that a wide variety of insects, including parasitoids and predators beneficial to the ecosystem, is essential to preserving ecological equilibrium. Integrated Pest Management (IPM) emphasizes a comprehensive strategy strategically integrating cultural, mechanical, biological, and chemical controls. This contrasts the traditional approach of chemical interventions as the beginning line of defense.

Cultural practices are the cornerstone of an effective strategy for controlling pests in tea gardens. An environment less conducive to spreading illnesses and pests can be created by implementing proper cleanliness, regular trimming, and removing waste and fallen leaves. Gardens that are well-maintained and have sufficient space between plants allow for adequate air circulation and lower the likelihood of fungal diseases. A proactive and responsive strategy for pest control involves monitoring the garden for signs of pest infestations and executing appropriate interventions based on observations. Both of these activities contribute to the monitoring of the garden.

Mechanical controls are critical to limit the risks posed by pests in tea gardens. Reduced reliance on chemical treatments can be achieved through the physical eradication of pests through methods such as handpicking or the utilization of instruments such as water sprays. Traps, barriers, and nets are all valuable methods for preventing pests from getting to the tea plants throughout the growing season. Mechanical controls not only provide focused solutions but also reduce the impact on beneficial insects, promoting an approach to pest management that is more sustainable and kind to the environment.

Biological controls control pest populations by utilizing the strength of the natural predators and parasites found in nature. Several beneficial insects feed on typical tea pests. Some examples of these insects are ladybugs, lacewings, predatory mites, and parasitic wasps. Establishing a balanced environment in which pest populations are naturally regulated can be accomplished by introducing and supporting the presence of natural predators. A healthier and more resilient tea garden can be achieved by implementing this strategy using the ecological principles of sustainability and decreasing the need for chemical pesticides.

Even though cultural, mechanical, and biological controls are the fundamental components of pest management in tea gardening, there are situations in which chemical treatments can be required. In situations like these, the prudent application of pesticides, by the standards and precautions that are advised, can be of assistance in containing the spread of pests. The selection of pesticides, on the other hand, ought to be done with caution, taking into consideration their impact on beneficial insects, the health of the soil, and the ecosystem as a whole. Targeted applications, as opposed to broad-spectrum treatments, reduce the amount of collateral damage caused to species that are not the intended targets.

Controlling diseases in tea gardens involves managing the dangers of various pathogens, including bacterial, viral, and fungal infections. Blister blight, gray mold, root rot, and several kinds of rust and mildew are among the most common diseases affecting tea. Humidity is particularly conducive to the growth of fungal infections; therefore, preventative measures are essential to avoid outbreaks. Several factors contribute to reducing conditions that are conducive to the formation and transmission of illnesses. These factors include proper sanitation, pruning, and keeping enough distance between tea plants.

In the same way pesticides are tools in the disease control arsenal, fungicides are also instruments; nevertheless, their application should be made with prudence and constraint. The use of fungicides should be predicated on careful monitoring and identifying particular illnesses. A reduction in the humidity levels conducive to the growth of fungi can be achieved by using cultural activities that encourage air circulation. These procedures include strategic trimming and adequate spacing. Neem oil and copper-based solutions are two examples of organic fungicides that provide alternatives that align with environmentally responsible farming methods.

Both in managing diseases and controlling pests, the ideas of integrated solutions are brought to the forefront more frequently. Crop rotation, the selection of disease-resistant tea cultivars, and the inclusion of disease-free planting material all contribute to developing resilience in the tea garden. A proactive strategy for disease management includes crucial components such as monitoring for early indicators of illnesses, promptly removing sick plant material, and adopting preventive measures during susceptible periods.

Environmental elements, such as climate and weather conditions, play a crucial role in determining the incidence of pests and diseases and the severity of their symptoms. At the same time that dry times can lead to stress and an increased vulnerability to pests, wet and humid temperatures generate conditions ideal for spreading fungal diseases. Observing the patterns of the weather and making adjustments to pest and In this way, tea enthusiasts can match their efforts with the dynamic character of their local environment so that disease management techniques can be appropriately implemented.

Regarding tea gardening, taking a holistic approach to disease management and pest control goes beyond the immediate concerns of safeguarding plants. Within the garden context, it incorporates the overarching objective of fostering ecological balance, biodiversity, and sustainability. Tea fans can become stewards of an ecosystem where tea plants coexist with a wide variety of creatures, each of which plays a role in the intricate fabric of nature, by adopting the ideas of integrated pest control and putting them into practice.

Managing diseases and pests in tea gardens are dynamic processes that require a sophisticated understanding of the interactions between tea plants, pests, and the environment. In conclusion, tea gardening's pest control and disease management demand this understanding. Enthusiasts can protect the essence of tea while protecting the delicate balance of the garden environment if they adopt an integrated approach that strategically integrates cultural, mechanical, biological, and chemical controls. Not only does the process of cultivating tea become a quest for flavor and aroma, but it also becomes a dance of harmony with the forces of nature. The artistry of pest control and disease management is revealed in carefully tending to tea plants. This leaves an indelible mark on the leaves that will later be used to decorate the teapot and on the tradition that flourishes in the center of the tea garden.

CHAPTER V

Seasons and Harvesting

Understanding Tea Plant Growth Cycles

The journey of cultivating tea is a dance with nature, a symphony orchestrated by the intricate growth cycles of the Camellia sinensis plant. Each stage of the growth cycle, beginning with the sensitive sprouting of new shoots and continuing through the luxuriant expansion of foliage and the eventual harvest of tea leaves, contributes to the distinctive personality of the produced tea. This section goes into the fascinating world of tea plant life cycles, illuminating the stages of germination, vegetative growth, flowering, and dormancy. When people passionate about tea begin to cultivate their tea gardens, it is not only a practical necessity but also a profound connection with the essence of tea to be aware of these growth cycles.

Beginning with germination, a process that bears the promise of new life and the emergence of the first small tea shoots, the voyage begins with the beginning of the journey. A period of cold treatment that breaks dormancy and prepares the seeds for germination is known as stratification, and it is one of the processes that tea seedlings go through before they are planted. After being planted in soil that has been adequately prepared, the delicate dance of water, warmth, and light begins to emerge. The first appearance of cotyledons indicates the beginning of the life cycle of the tea plant. The transition from the vegetative development phase to the larval growth phase is marked by the appearance of these embryonic leaves, which give sustenance until the actual leaves appear.

A moment of exuberance and vitality, the vegetative growth phase, is when the tea plant invests its energy in establishing a robust structure consisting of stems, branches, and leaves. The plant's abundant growth characterizes this phase. This endeavor aims to lay a solid groundwork for future expansion and, ultimately, the manufacturing of high-quality tea leaves. When the plant is at this phase, pruning becomes a significant activity because it helps shape the architecture of the plant, encourages lateral branching, and helps maintain an open canopy that allows for optimal light penetration. In addition, vigorous vegetative growth builds the framework for a well-defined root system, which secures the tea plant firmly in the soil.

The flushes of new growth that culminate in the harvest of tea leaves are the most celebrated feature of tea plant growth. The vegetative phase is the phase that prepares the way for tea plant growth. The emergence of the first flush, characterized by youthful, fragile leaves and a delicate flavor profile, occurs due to the prolonging of sunlight throughout the spring. There is a lot of anticipation surrounding this flush, considered the highest possible level of quality and freshness in the world of tea. Subsequent flushes occur due to shifting environmental signals, each of which possesses distinctive traits influenced by elements such as the weather, the altitude, and the soil composition.

The flowering phase of the tea plant is an essential stage in its life cycle, even though it is not as much celebrated in the tea industry. In response to favorable conditions, tea plants respond by producing clusters of fragrant blooms that are modest in size. In tea production, the flowering stage is not the primary emphasis because the objective is to harvest the leaves rather than the blossoms. However, the flowering stage is appealing to the eye and offers insights into the reproductive features of the plant. Flowers can be found in clusters or as single blooms, and their colors can range from white to pinkish-white in various combinations.

The tea plants go through a period of dormancy, rest, and rejuvenation after the flushing and blooming stages have passed. Typically, dormancy occurs during the winter months, coinciding with a decrease in both the temperature and the number of daylight hours. The tea plant needs to go through this period of dormancy to maintain its general health. During this time, the plant can conserve energy, build its root system, and prepare for the subsequent growth period that will occur during the following growing season. The plant adjusts its concentration from above-ground activities to below-ground storage and resilience while in a dormant state.

A thorough appreciation for the environmental cues that influence each step of the growth cycle of tea plants is required to comprehend the complexities of the tea plant's life cycle. For the plant, the length of the day, the temperature, and the conditions of the soil all play the role of conductors, directing it through the sequence of germination, vegetative development, flowering, and dormancy. The delicate balance between these parameters determines the quality and characteristics of the tea produced. This creates a dynamic interplay between nature's clues and the stewardship the grower exercises.

To achieve a harmonious relationship with the growth cycles of tea plants, it is essential to engage in practices such as pruning, soil preparation, and water management, respectively. In the case of pruning, for example, it is not simply a method of shaping the plant but also a strategic intervention that determines the timing and strength of flushes. An environment conducive to robust vegetative growth and fosters the formation of a healthy root system is provided by soil that is well-drained and rich in organic matter. It is possible to ensure that tea plants receive sufficient hydration without succumbing to waterlogged circumstances or drought stress by implementing water management practices linked with each growth phase's individual requirements.

It is a collaboration between the care of the gardener and the plant's response to the rhythms of nature that the cultivation of tea becomes a dance with the seasons. When people who are passionate about tea begin the process of gaining an understanding of the growth cycles of tea plants, they develop a heightened awareness of the ebb and flow of life in the garden. All of these factors—the birth of new shoots, the lush expansion of foliage, the fleeting beauty of blooms, and the peaceful dormancy—contribute to the intricate tapestry of tea cultivation.

A profound connection with the essence of tea can be fostered by an awareness of the growth cycles of tea plants, which goes beyond the practical requirements of cultivation. During the dormant phase, the leaves that unfold in the first flush carry the vibrancy of spring, the flowers evoke the fleeting beauty of nature, and the dormancy period symbolizes the wisdom of rest and renewal. Through the intricate dance of development cycles, tea fans become growers and guardians of a tradition that respects the complex link between the tea plant and the environment in which it grows.

In conclusion, the gradually developing story of tea plants' development cycles is about life, resiliency, and the unchanging rhythm of nature. Each phase, beginning with the delicate moment of germination and continuing through the brilliant flushes, brief blossoms, and calm hibernation, contributes to the distinctive personality of the produced tea. Tea fans, when they engage with these growth cycles, enter into a profound dialogue with the essence of tea. They become storytellers in a narrative that spans the seasons and connects them with the journey of Camellia sinensis, which is a journey that has stood the test of time.

Harvesting Leaves for Fresh Tea

When it comes to the cultivation of tea, the harvest occasion is a significant turning point because it is at this time that the abundance of nature is meticulously gathered to craft the essence of tea. A refined art, a delicate dance involving timing, technique, and a comprehensive understanding of the growth cycles of the tea plant, the harvesting of leaves for fresh tea is a delicate dance. This section looks into the problematic process of harvesting fresh tea leaves. It investigates the elements that determine the timing of harvest, the various types of tea leaves sought after, and the ways tea enthusiasts take to ensure a plentiful and high- quality production.

When it comes to harvesting tea leaves, timing is of the utmost importance, and it is inextricably tied to the growth cycles of the tea plant. Regarding tea harvesting, the first flush, distinguished by the appearance of sensitive, young leaves in the early spring, is sometimes regarded as the highest possible quality. The time of this initial harvest and the timing of the plant's response to rising daylight and warming temperatures have been meticulously engineered to match one another. Because they have recently emerged from their winter slumber, the young leaves of the first flush have a delicate flavor profile and are highly valued for their freshness.

Throughout the growing season, several flushes occur, each of which possesses its distinct collection of qualities formed by environmental variables, regional terroir, and the particular cultivar of the tea plant. The second flush produces More mature leaves, which occurs later in the spring or early in the summer. These leaves are more developed than the leaves produced by the first flush. These leaves may have a different flavor character, typically more robust and profound, even though they are still highly sought after. The third flush and the autumnal flush each bring additional differences, with the changing environmental cues mirrored in the leaves aroma, flavor, and look.

There is also a difference in the harvesting date based on the sort of tea being produced. The leaves of green tea are often harvested early in the growing season when they are still young and contain a high concentration of chlorophyll. Green tea is renowned for its freshness and vitality. An infusion that is vivid green in color has a grassy, vegetal flavor profile and is frequently slightly sweet is the result of this. Typically, white tea is gathered during the first flush of the year, when the buds are still covered in fine white hairs, which gives it a distinctive appearance and a delicate flavor. White tea is distinguished by its little processing and the use of young leaves and buds.

It is necessary to take a more subtle approach to harvesting oolong teas because of their vast range of oxidation degrees. Oolongs that have undergone light oxidation may be harvested sooner in the growing season to capture the freshness of young leaves. On the other hand, oolongs that have experienced more significant oxidation may be picked later to allow the leaves to develop more nuanced flavors. As a result of the whole oxidation process that black teas go through, they are typically collected later in the season when the leaves have reached their full maturity. This results in a darker infusion and a more robust flavor profile.

When collecting tea leaves, the methodology is just as important as the timing, with individual techniques producing diverse outcomes. The labor-intensive yet renowned art of hand plucking entails choosing individual leaves or leaf buds by hand cautiously and methodically. This technique is the method of choice for teas of superior quality, particularly those in which the delicate nature of the leaves is of the utmost importance. Hand plucking provides greater precision in selecting only the desired leaves, which guarantees a harvest that is both consistent and of high quality.

On the other hand, machine harvesting is more mechanical and involves the simultaneous harvesting of vast parts of the tea plant. It is generally more appropriate for mass-produced teas, where a slightly coarser quality is acceptable, even though this method is efficient and cost-effective for tea production. Machine harvesting is frequently used when it comes to teas like CTC (Crush, Tear, Curl) black tea, where uniformity and consistency are favored over the intricacies of leaf selection. This method may result in a mixture of leaves, stems, and buds.

Those passionate about tea also consider the plucking standard, which refers to the number of leaves and the presence of buds harvested during each plucking. The two leaves and a bud standard are typical for producing high-quality teas. This standard involves the young, sensitive leaves and the unopened bud being simultaneously plucked together. This standard is typically associated with the artisanal manufacturing of premium teas because it guarantees a well-balanced flavor profile through its use.

In addition to the technical components of harvesting, the person's attitude is a significant factor in determining the quality of the leaves received. The skillful harvesting process requires careful handling, a keen eye for the subtleties of each tea bush, and an understanding of the unique requirements of each flush. All of these factors contribute to the high level of artistry involved. The delicate nature of the leaves is respected by the harvester, who uses a gentle touch to ensure that the leaves arrive in the best possible shape at the processing stage.

A number of factors determine the quality of the harvest, one of which is the placement of the plucking on the tea bush. Apical leaves, located at the tip of the tea shoot, are frequently selected because they are soft and have a concentrated flavor. The leaves get slightly more mature as the stalk continues to extend, which may change the flavor and aroma of the leaves. In producing certain teas, such as certain white teas, the bud or the first two leaves may be harvested only, while the larger, more mature leaves are discarded.

The leaves that have been picked are then sent through the next stage of their journey, which is the processing stage, after the precise ballet of timing and precision that takes place in the tea garden. The processing procedures, including withering, rolling, oxidation, and drying, are significant in determining the tea's final properties. The choices made during the harvesting process, such as the time and plucking standard, lay the groundwork for the subsequent processing procedures and contribute to the overall quality and flavor profile of the tea produced.

Many people who are passionate about tea take great pleasure in the act of harvesting, regardless of whether they are growing their own tea garden or obtaining leaves from established plantations. There is a moment of connection with the earth, a celebration of the plant's life, and a communion with the time-honored custom of making tea. They take part in a ritual that acknowledges the essence of tea, the delicate, living leaves that carry the promise of flavor, perfume, and a trip that spans the seasons. This ritual occurs as the hands pluck the leaves, whether delicately by hand or efficiently by machine.

In conclusion, collecting leaves to make fresh tea is a significant act that establishes a connection between cultivation and consumption. The hands of harvesters become storytellers, weaving the narrative of each flush, each leaf, and each cup of tea. It is a choreography of timing, technique, and tradition. It is a ballet that involves the hands of harvesters. The delicate dance with nature, which is driven by the growth cycles of the tea plant, unfolds in the precise selection of leaves, which has the effect of sculpting the character of the tea that will adorn the teapot and, ultimately, the discerning palate of tea fans all around the world.

Drying and Processing Your Own Tea

The intricate dance with nature enters a new step as the sun-kissed leaves of the tea plant are gently harvested from the garden. This new phase is the art of drying and processing the tea. The process of transforming newly collected tea leaves into a finished product ready to be brewed is an art rooted in tradition, innovation, and an intimate awareness of the flavor profiles that are wanted. This section looks into the fascinating realm of drying and processing your tea, examining the numerous ways utilized, the impact these procedures have on flavor and scent, and the role of craftsmanship in determining the personality of the finished infusion.

The moment of harvest, characterized by the gentle plucking of tender leaves, is the beginning of a journey that goes beyond the tea garden and into the processing domain. Processing is done primarily to halt the natural enzymatic activity within the leaves, avoid further oxidation, and ensure that the ideal attributes of the tea are maintained despite the process. Drying, rolling, oxidation, and burning are some of the most critical procedures tea connoisseurs go through to create a product that reflects both the garden's terroir and the harvester's intention.

The initial phase in tea processing is called drying, and its purpose is to reduce the amount of moisture contained within the leaves. This lays the groundwork for subsequent transformations. How the tea is dried ultimately significantly influences the flavor, aroma, and appearance of the finished product. Traditional methods include sun-drying, which involves laying out freshly picked leaves in the open air so they can wilt in the sun's warmth. The tea is given a subtle and delicate character through this process, which, albeit time-consuming, enables the leaves to wither and gradually acquire rich flavors.

The processing of modern tea frequently involves the use of mechanical drying processes to complete the process more quickly and achieve higher consistency. The reduction of moisture can be accomplished more expediently and regulated through electric dryers, hot air ovens, and other controlled settings. Although these methods are effective, they can potentially modify the flavor profile compared to sun-drying. As a result, tea fans need to use caution when selecting the drying method that corresponds with the end they want to achieve.

In addition, the process of drying that is selected differs from one kind of tea to another. The drying process for green teas, renowned for their crispness and vivid green color, often involves pan-firing or steaming. Green teas are praised for their freshness and vibrant green color. In the process of pan-firing, the leaves are transferred to a hot wok, where they are allowed to wither and acquire a somewhat burnt flavor. Steaming is a widespread method in Japan, and it involves using hot steam to prevent oxidation and provide a particular umami flavor to the tea.

To preserve the delicate nuances of the leaves, white teas, already noted for their little processing, are often dried using air or sun drying. Oolong teas, found in a wide range of oxidation degrees, can be dried using various methods to obtain the flavor profile customers want. It is possible to roast darker oolongs to enhance their depth, whereas lighter oolongs can be exposed to moderate drying to preserve their flowery or fruity aromas.

The final product's appearance, aroma, and general presentation are all significant factors influenced by rolling or shape, which is another essential phase in tea manufacturing. The goal is to break down the cellular structure of the leaves, which will result in the release of enzymes and essential oils that add to the flavor profile. To achieve more nuanced control over the rolling process, hand-rolling, which is a traditional method that is frequently used for producing high-quality teas, is commonly used. By carefully shaping the leaves into twists or curls, the leaves can maintain their integrity while also contributing to the aesthetic attractiveness of the tea.

When it comes to large-scale production, where efficiency and consistency are of the utmost importance, machine rolling, a more mechanized process, is traditionally utilized. Machine processing provides uniformity and may be tailored to meet the unique requirements of various types of tea, even though it may lose some of the artisanal touch usually associated with hand-rolling. In the end, the decision between hand-rolling and machine-rolling becomes a reflection of the producer's mindset and the features sought in the finished tea.

The leaves are subjected to oxygen to facilitate the initiation of enzymatic reactions during the oxidation process, which is an essential stage in the preparation of some varieties of tea. To differentiate green, oolong, and black teas, which all fall along a range of oxidation levels, this procedure differentiates them from one another. Green teas are subjected to a small amount of oxidation, which helps them maintain their delicate flavor and brilliant green color. Oolong teas, which have varied degrees of oxidation, display various tastes, ranging from fruity and floral to toasted and powerful. Fully oxidized black teas produce darker hues, fuller bodies, and more nuanced flavor profiles than their unoxidized counterparts.

The oxidation process is typically accomplished by a regulated procedure in which the leaves are spread out in an atmosphere with adequate ventilation. This allows oxygen to interact with the enzymes in the leaves. The length of time that the tea is allowed to oxidize is a crucial component that plays a role in determining the final product. To monitor the leaves as they change color, scent, and flavor, it is necessary to have a deep comprehension of the intentions of the tea maker and the qualities sought in the tea being created.

The final phase in tea processing is known as "firing" or "roasting," it is responsible for ending oxidation and further characterizing the flavor profile. This phase includes exposing the leaves to heat, which can be accomplished by various means, such as roasting them in the oven, pan-firing them, or tumbling them in a heated drum. There is a correlation between the intensity of the firing process and the depth and complexity of the tea. Lighter roasts preserve more delicate flavors, while darker roasts give a more robust and toasted character during the firing process.

The selection of the firing process is also based on regional customs and the tea style intended to be produced. For instance, Chinese teas frequently have a range of roasting levels, enabling a wide variety of flavors to be contained within a single tea. On the other hand, certain Japanese green teas, such as Sencha, are renowned for their steaming processing, which helps maintain a bright and grassy quality without roasting.

When it comes to drying and processing your tea, craftsmanship carries a significant amount of weight. Individuals passionate about tea become custodians of flavor, scent, and the delicate dance between nature and technique, regardless of whether centuries-old traditions or innovative ways guide them. The decisions made during each stage of the processing process create a canvas for self-expression and an embodiment of the tea maker's vision. These decisions range from the selection of the drying method to the length of time that the tea is allowed to oxidize and the degree of roasting.

An entire story is told in every cup of tea prepared with hand-processed tea, beginning with the harvest and ending with the infusion. The rich tapestry of flavors and scents that fascinate tea connoisseurs results from several factors, including the rhythm of withering leaves, the skill of rolling and shaping, the alchemy of oxidation, and the final kiss of heat in fire. As individuals embark on processing their tea, they become not only cultivators but also artists. They guide the leaves through a transformative journey that culminates in the pleasurable experience of consuming a cup of tea that they have produced themselves.

It is important to note that drying and processing your own tea is a celebration of history and creativity. In this process, the hands of the tea maker become conduits of flavor and stewards of terroir. Every stage of the process, from drying to rolling, oxidation to burning, is like a brushstroke on the canvas of tea, catching the essence of the leaves and the intention of the person who harvested them. As people passionate about tea begin to investigate the world of tea processing, they go on a voyage of discovery, creativity, and a profound connection with the age-old craft that converts freshly picked leaves into a symphony of flavors in a cup of tea.

CHAPTER VI

Creating a Relaxing Tea Space

Designing a Cozy Tea Corner

Within the frenetic rhythm of modern life, the acquisition of moments of peace and connection has become an increasingly valuable commodity. The concept of a cozy tea corner has gained popularity as tea lovers seek comfort in preparing and savoring their beverage. Not only does the idea of designing a facility solely dedicated to tea enrich the experience, but it also creates a sanctuary for relaxation and contemplation. This section delves into the art of constructing a pleasant tea area, diving into aspects such as location, atmosphere, furniture, and decorations, as well as the profound influence of creating a personalized sanctuary for the enjoyment of tea.

The first thing that needs to be done to create a warm tea area is to choose the ideal destination. In a perfect world, this location would be a serene hideaway that provides a momentary reprieve from the pressures and responsibilities of everyday life. The sunshine through windows may lend warmth and vibrancy to the tea area. Therefore, it is essential to take into consideration the natural light that is present. It is recommended that you select a spot that offers a view, whether it be a garden, a cityscape, or even just a corner of a room containing a piece of artwork you particularly enjoy. Creating an environment in which one can feel connected to the environment while also relishing the sensory experience of tea is the purpose of this endeavor.

The atmosphere of the tea corner is significantly influenced by the present atmosphere. An ordinary room can be transformed into a warm and inviting hideaway by incorporating lighting, color schemes, and design into the overall environment. Lighting that is mild and warm is desirable since it creates an atmosphere that is calm and inviting. Consider adding table lamps, string lights, or candles to generate a calming glow. To create a quiet and uncomplicated atmosphere, it is common practice to use earthy and neutral hues for a tea area. Adding character and a sense of individuality to a place can be accomplished through personal touches such as artwork, wall decals, or even a small shelf of books.

To ensure both comfort and functionality, the selection of furnishings for a tea area is of the utmost importance. It is crucial to have a comfy chair or additional padded seating, as this will provide a cozy place to relax and unwind. With the help of a small table or tea cart, you can create a surface suitable for brewing necessities, awareness, and possibly even a few treasured decorations. The furniture must be organized to allow easy movement and access to the tea instruments. This will ensure that the experience of drinking tea is smooth and delightful. Consider the possibility of introducing natural components into the area, such as bamboo or wood furniture, to enhance the organic and peaceful atmosphere.

Infusing the tea area with personality and charm is accomplished through accessories and decor, which are the final touches. A shelf or cabinet specifically designed to store a curated assortment of teas, teapots, and cups may be included in a tea nook. Texture and warmth can be added to a space through decorative elements such as throws, cushions, and rugs. The presence of plants or fresh flowers adds a touch of nature to the area, bringing vitality and vigor. The objective is to design a space that exudes warmth and friendliness, characterized by an atmosphere in which every component shows admiration and affection for the art of tea.

Awareness is, without a doubt, the most critical

component of a warm and inviting tea corner. If you choose teapots, cups, and other accessories that align with your personal preferences, you will have a more enjoyable experience overall. When selecting a teapot, it is essential to consider the popular forms of tea consumed. Teapots made of robust clay are ideal for brewing oolongs and black teas. At the same time, delicate porcelain or ceramic teaware is a perfect accompaniment to the ritual of brewing green or white teas. Make sure to get high-quality tea cups that are comfortable to handle and display the colors and fragrances of the tea made. It is also possible to add a practical and aesthetic component to the tea nook by selecting a high-quality tea tray or mat.

Storage solutions are an essential component in keeping

a clean tea area that is well-organized and clear of clutter. When maintaining a lovely arrangement of teaware, tea leaves, and accessories, consider shelving, cabinets, or trays. The use of transparent containers to store different types of tea helps maintain their freshness and contributes to the aesthetic appeal of the space. Not only does a tea area that is well-organized and visually appealing contribute to the overall sense of order and tranquility, but it also contributes to the aesthetic aspect of the situation.

When it comes to building a pleasant tea corner,

personalization is an essential component. Embrace the space with elements that reflect individual interests, tastes, and the cultural influences that have shaped it. Display works of art, photos, or other artifacts with significant sentimental meaning. To create an atmosphere that is diverse and welcoming to people of all backgrounds, consider including items from many cultures, such as traditional tea sets, textiles, or artwork. The tea corner is a canvas for self-expression, and every detail should resonate with the tea enthusiast's identity and journey with tea. The tea corner must be beautifully decorated.

In the design process, utility ought to be prioritized in addition to aesthetics as the most crucial consideration. Take the necessary steps to ensure the tea corner is stocked with everything required for a smooth brewing experience. A dependable kettle or hot water dispenser, a selection of teas that can be adapted to fit a variety of moods, and essential accessories such as a teapot, infusers, and high-quality water are all included in this product. An area designated explicitly for trash disposal, such as a small bin or an option for composting, helps make the design more practical. The tea area is transformed into a well-rounded space that cultivates both the senses and the art of tea preparation when designed to showcase its aesthetic and functional qualities.

Not only does the creation of a comfortable tea area involve the physical architecture of the space, but it also involves the cultivation of a mindful and present mindset. The practice of mindfulness could be included in the routine of drinking tea. Some examples of mindfulness practices include attentive breathing, meditation, or just relishing each sip with focused attention. Creating a tea area that serves not only as a place to sip tea but also as a place to cultivate a more profound connection with the here and now is that of a sanctuary. The tea area transforms into a portal to a moment of tranquility amid the hustle and bustle of everyday life as the fragrant steam rises from the teapot and the tastes dance on the palate.

In conclusion, building a pleasant tea corner is a delightful undertaking involving more than just designing the furniture and choosing the decorations. Creating a haven for tea enthusiasts is a creative process that involves incorporating elements of aesthetics, utility, and personal expression into the design of the space. When establishing a space where one can appreciate not just tea but also moments of tranquility, introspection, and connection with the essence of life, each decision contributes to the art of creating a space. This includes the choice of location and atmosphere, the selection of teaware, and the incorporation of personal touches. Slowing down, embracing simplicity, and discovering joy in drinking tea are all beautiful things, and the cozy tea area becomes a tribute to the beauty of these things.

Incorporating Decorative Elements

The art of tea is not merely a beverage ritual but a sensory journey that engages sight, smell, touch, and taste. Constructing a room solely devoted to tea entails more than just the technical aspects of brewing; it is also an opportunity to create an atmosphere that invigorates the senses and encourages a sense of calmness. This section delves into the complex world of introducing artistic elements into your tea room. We investigate the impact that color, texture, artwork, and thematic accents have on enhancing the aesthetics and enriching the overall experience of drinking tea.

The palette that you select for your tea place is the one that will determine the mood and atmosphere of the entire experience. Color has a significant impact on both mood and atmosphere. Subdued and soft tones, such as greens, blues, and earthy neutrals, produce a soothing and comforting ambiance, and they resonate with the natural aspects typically associated with tea. The brilliant hues of tea leaves and the delicate colors of infusions can take center stage thanks to the presence of these colors, which generate a sense of tranquility and give a visually calming backdrop. Alternately, vibrant and warm hues such as reds or rich oranges can fill the area with vitality, producing a more dynamic and energizing setting. Your choice of color allows you to express yourself personally and reflects the ambiance you want to make for your tea rituals.

The sensory experience of your tea corner can be enhanced by the involvement of texture, which plays a tactile role. Soft, fluffy cushions or throws incorporated into seating arrangements provide an atmosphere conducive to relaxation and comfort. A tactile richness that aligns with the organic essence of tea can be achieved through natural materials such as wood, bamboo, or woven fabrics. Another way to add texture to the environment is by selecting teaware; whether it be smooth porcelain, rough clay, or delicate glass, each option offers a different kind of tactile sensation. Your setting for drinking tea can be transformed into a multisensory refuge by incorporating a variety of textures, which will invite touch as an additional layer of engagement in the ritual.

A visual narrative that is in tune with the essence of tea may be created by incorporating artwork and decorative elements into your tea area. This will infuse your tea corner with personality and character. Consider the possibility of combining pieces that are in harmony with your aesthetic and that inspire a sense of calm. Your tea environment can be transformed into a curated gallery of visual delights by incorporating focus points such as traditional Chinese or Japanese artwork, posters inspired by nature, or even a gallery wall of tea-related images. Not only does the painting serve as a decorative feature, it also serves as a storytelling component that elevates the space above its plain functional capabilities.

Individuals are given the option to exhibit their unique passions and interests within the tea room through the use of thematic accents. Multiple layers of depth and meaning are added by theme components, regardless of whether a particular culture, historical time, or artistic movement inspires them. As an illustration, a tea area with Zen influences might have a minimalistic set of furnishings, bonsai plants, and a soothing rock garden. An alternative might be for a tea room with a vintage motif to display vintage prints, lace doilies, and antique teapots. Your tea corner can become a mirror of your one-of-a-kind aesthetic tastes and a voyage into a universe that connects with your spirit if you incorporate thematic accents into it.

Lighting is an essential component that plays a significant role in boosting the atmosphere of your tea place. A warm and inviting glow is produced by soft and diffused lighting, making it an excellent choice for promoting a sense of comfort and relaxation. If you want to generate a subtle illumination that matches the peaceful nature of tea rituals, consider including table lamps, string lights, or even candles. If accessible, natural light brings an organic and dynamic quality to the area, resulting in an active play of shadows and highlights that vary during the day. When light interacts with one another, it becomes an essential component of the sensory experience, enhancing the visual appeal of your tea area.

Adding plants to your tea place infuses it with a sense of nature and gives it a sense of vitality and brightness. A dynamic and living aspect may be introduced by selecting potted plants or fresh flowers. This element not only adds to an improvement in aesthetics but also helps to contribute to a sense of well-being. In addition, the sensory experience can be further elevated by the presence of plants that emit calming scents, such as jasmine or lavender. A pleasant setting that is in harmony with the spirit of tea as a celebration of the natural world is created when greenery is present. This facilitates a connection with nature and creates a harmonious environment.

Adding a sense of ceremony and reverence to your tea area can be accomplished by using ceremonial components derived from traditional tea ceremonies from various traditions. This may contain a specific location for a tea ceremony set comprising a Japanese chai arrangement or a Chinese gongfu tea ceremony arrangement. The ritualistic quality of tea preparation can be enhanced by incorporating components such as a tea table, tea equipment, and even a simple gong into the process. Not only do the ceremonial aspects serve as practical instruments, they also serve as symbolic symbols of the mindfulness and intention associated with tea ceremonies.

Your teaware collection can be displayed and organized with the help of storage options, which constitute a design feature in and of themselves. Displaying teapots, cups, and accessories as ornamental elements can be accomplished through open shelving or cabinets with glass fronts. Tea leaves can be stored in see-through containers, which adds to the aesthetic value of the space and contributes to the overall aesthetic. Incorporating storage options that align with the design theme ensures that your tea corner continues to be functional and aesthetically beautiful.

The thoughtful addition of treasured things and personal touches enhances your tea place's cozy and one-of-a-kind nature. This is true whether it is a cherished teapot handed down from generation to generation, a ceramic cup handcrafted, or a collection of tea-themed trinkets; all of these artifacts infuse the room with personal history and emotional relevance. Your tea area will mirror your journey with tea if you surround yourself with meaningful objects. This will create a space that experiences a profound sense of personalization and comfort.

In conclusion, including ornamental elements in your tea environment provides an opportunity for creative exploration beyond brewing tea's practical features. Creating an atmosphere that appeals to the senses, conveys a visual narrative, and resonates with one's unique identity is called aesthetic curation. Various elements, including the color palette, textures, thematic accents, and lighting, influence the tea environment's aesthetics. You may transform your tea corner into a sanctuary that honors the beauty, artistry, and mindfulness inherent in the world of tea by adding decorative items. This will change it from a simple location to prepare tea into a celebration of these qualities.

Choosing the Right Furniture and Accessories

Designing a tea environment goes beyond the simple act of boiling tea; it is about creating a sanctuary that invites one to slow down, relish the moment, and immerse oneself in the ritual of drinking tea. One of the most critical aspects of this design process is choosing the appropriate furniture and accessories for the tea corner. These elements are essential in determining the tea corner's overall beauty, as well as its utility and comfort requirements. In the following paragraphs, we will explore the factors and nuances that should be considered when selecting the appropriate furniture and accessories. We will also investigate how each component contributes to the development of a tea haven that is both cozy and harmonious.

The seating arrangement is the most critical factor in determining how pleasant a tea room is. The selection of seating significantly impacts the overall experience, regardless of whether it is set apart as a secluded nook for private contemplation or as a public area for drinking tea with loved ones. A comfy chair or cushioned seating encourages relaxation and makes it possible to settle in and take pleasure in the peace of the present moment. Please consider the ergonomics and dimensions of the seating to ensure that it is suitable for the tasks that will be performed in the area. Floor cushions or poufs offer a more comfortable alternative for individuals who like a more casual and private environment. Creating a seating arrangement that is attractive, favorable to contemplation, and well-suited for the chosen method of tea consumption is the objective of this project.

Regarding brewing necessities, awareness, and a few decorative accents, the tables and surfaces in a tea area serve as valuable platforms. Whether you go with a table, a tea cart, or even just a basic tray, it comes down to the available room and the look you want. A tea table with a large surface area allows for the arrangement of teapots, cups, and accessories, making the process of preparing tea more streamlined. The mobility and flexibility offered by tea carts make it simple to transfer teaware and refreshments that are being served. To achieve a more natural and peaceful atmosphere in the area, it is recommended to use raw materials such as bamboo or wood. The dimensions and height of the table must complement the seating arrangement to help create a sense of harmony and equilibrium.

Shelving and storage solutions are three necessary components when keeping a tea room orderly and visually appealing. Open shelves or cabinets can house a handpicked assortment of teas, teapots, and accessories, thereby changing storage into a display containing attractive elements. The use of transparent containers to store tea leaves not only helps maintain their freshness but also contributes to the aesthetic appeal of the space. It is also possible for shelves to function as a platform for thematic accents, plants, or sentimental things, all of which contribute to the particular character of the area. Ensure that storage solutions contribute to the overall design rather than detracting from it by striking a healthy balance between aesthetics and usefulness. This is the key to a practical storage solution.

Accessories are an essential component when it comes to decorating the tea room with personality, functionality, and thematic accents. High-quality teaware, including teapots, cups, and infusers, serves a dual purpose: it is functional and aesthetically pleasing. When trying to achieve a cohesive look, it is essential to consider the accessories' material, style, and craftsmanship. Creating a visually captivating tableau can be accomplished by coordinating sets or mixing and combining different styles. Additionally, accessories like a tea tray, coasters, or a timer contribute to a more refined and delightful brewing experience. These accessories enhance the functioning of the tea room and have the potential to make the experience more enjoyable. The area is enriched with additional levels of meaning and storytelling when adorned with thematic accessories, such as cultural or seasonal items.

The lighting in a tea room is an element that is sometimes overlooked despite its transformational potential. Having the appropriate lighting not only illuminates the brewing process but also helps to set the mood and enhance the atmosphere. It is better to have soft and diffused lighting since it produces a warm and inviting glow that complements the peaceful environment that tea rituals provide. Soft illumination can be achieved by strategically positioning table lamps, floor lamps, or even string lights to achieve the desired effect. If natural light is present, it contributes a dynamic and organic component, making it possible for the play of sunlight to become an essential component of the sensory experience. A visually engaging and calming setting is created due to the interaction between light and shadow, which contributes to the overall aesthetic ambiance.

Adding a layer of comfort and flair to the tea environment is accomplished through textiles and soft furnishings. Not only can cushions, throws, and rugs contribute to the overall aesthetics of the seating area, but they also increase the tactile experience of the seated space. Materials made from natural materials, such as cotton or linen, give off an air of ease and simplicity. Think about using textiles that have patterns or colors that are soothing and that are in line with the atmosphere you want to create in the room. Not only do these soft furnishings contribute to the physical comfort of the room, but they also provide an opportunity to include texture, color, and warmth into the design, creating an environment that encourages one to linger and relax.

Plants and vegetation bring A touch of nature into the tea place, contributing to the space's freshness, energy, and aesthetic appeal. This can be accomplished by carefully placing fresh flowers or potted plants on tables or shelves or even hanging them from the ceiling to create a link with the natural environment. In addition to contributing to the sensory experience, plants that emit relaxing aromas, such as lavender or chamomile, also contribute to the general enhancement of the atmosphere. By the natural and holistic philosophy frequently connected with tea ceremonies, greenery contributes to developing a sense of well-being and tranquility.

To enhance the storytelling component of the tea environment, it is beneficial to incorporate cultural or thematic elements into the furniture and accessories. Whether they are influenced by classic European tearooms, traditional tea ceremonies from East Asia, or personal cultural history, these aspects add complexity and meaning to the whole experience. To create a thematic cohesion that resonates with the spirit of tea as a worldwide and diverse heritage, it is possible to choose furniture types, accessories, and decorative objects to reflect a particular cultural aesthetic. The tea environment transforms from merely a practical place into a curated expression of identity and respect for tea culture when cultural aspects are incorporated.

Personalization is the key to success when it comes to creating a genuine tea area that is deeply tied to one's tastes. It is possible to add to the one-of-a-kind quality of the area by incorporating nostalgic things, cherished awareness, or even accessories that have been handcrafted. Through the incorporation of personal touches, the tea area is transformed from a generic environment into a profoundly personal refuge. The area is imbued with a sense of personal history and warmth when it contains items with emotional meaning, such as a family heirloom or a gift from a close friend. It is possible to transform one's tea area into a mirror of one's journey with tea and a source of comfort and joy by surrounding oneself with artifacts that bear personal significance.

To summarize, selecting the appropriate furniture and accessories is a process that is not only intentional but also complex, and it goes beyond only taking into account practical factors. Specifically, it entails the creation of an environment that harmoniously combines aesthetics, utility, and comfort to improve the whole experience of drinking tea. The design narrative is shaped by each component, which includes the seating arrangement, the tables, the storage solutions, and the accessories. The result is a tea environment that encourages tranquility, reflection, and a more profound connection with the ritual of tea drinking. Carefully selecting furniture and accessories becomes a form of artistic expression for tea enthusiasts as they construct their tea haven. This transforms a corner of a room into a sanctuary that is a haven for calm and sensory delight.

CHAPTER VII

Exploring Tea Blends and Flavors

Introduction to Tea Blending

With its rich tapestry of flavors and aromas, tea has captivated enthusiasts' palates for centuries. Despite this, the world of tea encompasses more than just single-origin brews, and it invites those who enjoy tea to explore the artistic realm of mixing. Tea blending is a craft that involves the thoughtful combining of various types of tea, herbs, spices, and botanicals to make personalized infusions that appeal to the preferences and palates of specific customers. This section will examine the art and science behind tea blending. We will uncover the complexities, procedures, and fulfilling processes of producing individualized blends that honor the diversity within the tea world.

Tea blending, at its core, is a symphony of flavors, a harmonious collaboration of many materials that are painstakingly arranged to generate a balanced and enjoyable composition. One of the critical reasons for blending tea is the aspiration to produce a beverage that surpasses a single variety's intrinsic qualities. This is accomplished by combining distinct profiles to make a cup of tea that is singular and complex. As a result of this procedure, tea blenders become comparable to perfumers, picking and blending various components to produce a sensory experience that is more than the sum of its parts. This technique facilitates an infinite amount of creativity.

One of the most important aspects of tea blending is the availability of various teas, each with its characteristics. Numerous blends are built on the foundation of black, green, white, oolong, and pu-erh teas, each providing diverse flavors, colors, and scents to the overall composition. The robust and fully oxidized black teas contribute malty aromas and deep caramel color to the mixes that they are used in. As a result of their fresh and grassy flavors, green teas contribute a sense of brightness and a lighter liquor. White teas, which are delicate and undergo minimum processing, provide a trace of sweetness and flowery nuances to the beverage. Oolongs, characterized by their partial oxidation, come in various flavors, ranging from fruity and fragrant to toasted and complex. After being matured and fermented, pu-erh teas bring earthy and mellow tones to blends, which adds depth to the overall experience.

When it comes to tea mixing, herbs and botanicals play a crucial role because they offer various flavors, fragrances, and combinations of medicinal properties. Some of the most common selections include Mint, chamomile, lavender, and hibiscus, which can offer a sense of freshness, relaxing qualities, or brilliant hues to an overall blend. Cinnamon, ginger, cardamom, and cloves impart warmth, depth, and a hint of exotic charm to what they are used in. The addition of fruits, whether they are fresh or dried, imparts a burst of fruity aromas, as well as sweetness and acidity. Because there is a wide range of alternatives, tea blenders can create a palette of components that corresponds with their vision and the outcome they want the blend to produce.

To master the art of tea blending, it is not enough to combine the components randomly; rather, one must have a profound comprehension of the qualities and interactions of various components. The expertise comes in developing a harmonious balance in which no single element dominates, allowing each component to add its distinctive qualities to the overall composition. When blending, it is essential for blenders to consider various criteria, including the intensity of the flavor, the parameters of the brewing process, and the compatibility of the ingredients. A refined taste and a strong intuitive sense are necessary for this delicate dance.

When it comes to successfully blending tea, one of the most critical components is always giving careful thought to the flavor profiles. It is essential to thoroughly understand the various flavors and fragrances that the multiple teas and botanicals offer to the blend. Creating a morning blend that is both balanced and powerful can be accomplished, for example, by combining the malty richness of Assam black tea with the citrusy brightness of Ceylon or Darjeeling. Similarly, a pleasant and fragrant infusion can be produced by blending the floral undertones of jasmine green tea with the sweet and sour flavor of dried berries. Engaging in experimentation and exploration is essential, allowing the palate to direct the journey toward the ideal combination.

Regarding the blending process, one of the most critical aspects is choosing the base teas that will work as the canvas for the creation. As the infusion progresses, the base tea not only affects the blend's overall personality but also interacts with the other components throughout the process. As a result of their robust and bold characteristics, black teas are frequently selected as a solid basis for mixes that incorporate aspects of citrus, herbs, or spices. Green teas have a more delicate and vegetal flavor profile and are very well suited to be combined with flowery and fruity flavors. White teas, highly regarded for their understated nature, are well-suited for making blends designed to highlight the subtle interplay of flavors.

The actual process of mixing comes into play once the ingredients have been selected. This may be accomplished manually by combining the components in a predetermined ratio, ensuring that the flavors are distributed evenly. On the other hand, some tea blenders use machinery to attain consistency and precision in the manufacturing of vast quantities of tea. The blending process may also involve stacking several components, allowing each to keep its individuality until the end of the infusion process. The objective is to produce a blend that progressively reveals successive layers of flavor with each sip, showing the mix's complexity.

Blending tea, in addition to providing a palette for creative expression, also provides a canvas for the telling of stories. The cultural traditions, regional peculiarities, or personal tales of many people inspire many blends. As an illustration, a combination of Moroccan Mint may take consumers to the busy markets of Marrakech, or a mix of London Fog may conjure up the refined atmosphere of a British teatime. Blends with names such as "Harmony," "Serenity," or "Sunset Bliss" provide a feeling of the environment or experience that is supposed to be brought about. Every blend transforms into a sensory adventure, allowing tea lovers to journey through various landscapes and stories with every cup.

Additionally elevating the craft, the advent of artisanal and boutique tea blending has fostered a culture of research and invention, further boosting the craft. There has been a rebirth in the world of tea, which has been brought about by small-scale blenders who frequently deal with high-quality and ethically obtained ingredients. These artists stretch the boundaries of traditional blending by experimenting with unexpected combinations, uncommon botanicals, and limited-edition releases. As a result, they introduce tea fans to flavors that are both novel and thrilling. In response to this movement, there has been an increase in the demand for originality and a more profound connection with the origin and quality of the ingredients.

Blending tea is not exclusive to commercial manufacturers; instead, it is a beautiful activity that enthusiasts can engage in while sitting in the convenience of their own homes. Home blending allows people to create teas tailored to their specific preferences, experiment with different flavors, and share their creations with their loved ones and friends. A straightforward combination of black tea and dried lavender can create a soothing infusion for the evening, while a combination of green tea and citrus peels can provide a zesty pick-me-up after a long day. A significant amount of self-expression is involved in the process, in addition to creating the ideal cup.

The investigation of tea blending also encompasses the idea of "flavor pairing," which is selecting components based on the attributes that complement or contrast. Recognizing chemicals in various ingredients that complement or balance one another is the goal of this method, which was taken from the realm of culinary arts. Creating a harmonic and well-rounded combination can be accomplished, for instance, by combining the sweet tones of a honeybush herbal tea with the acidity of dried berries. Similarly, the earthy richness of pu-erh tea, when combined with the warmth of cinnamon and ginger, may generate a comforting and energizing experience.

To summarize, the process of blending tea is an enthralling adventure into the world of flavors and smells, as well as the boundless possibilities resulting from the combination of various ingredients. The art of tea blending celebrates the creativity, originality, and narrative inherent in the world of tea. Commercial producers, artisanal blenders, and home enthusiasts alike practice this skill. A sensory journey that encourages discovery and cultivates a deeper connection with the rich tapestry of the tea heritage is created by each blend, which transforms into a one-of-a-kind expression over time. It is a realm where the cup becomes a canvas, and every sip unfolds a story of craftsmanship, creativity, and the joyful pursuit of the perfect. Tea lovers join this realm when they go on the path of blending.

Experimenting with Different Flavors

The world of tea is a vast and diverse landscape, offering an array of flavors, aromas, and textures that cater to a myriad of preferences. For those passionate about the subject, the trip is not limited to the enjoyment of conventional mixes; rather, it entails the fascinating study of individual tastes and the excitement of experimenting with various flavors. The purpose of this section is to encourage tea lovers to venture outside of their comfort zones and embrace the enormous spectrum of possibilities that tea blending and taste experimentation offer. This section will examine the art and delight of injecting creativity into your tea experience.

Tea is an excellent beginning place for flavor exploration because of its inherent variety, which results from the many different cultivars, terroirs, and processing methods. Whether the robust and malty notes of Assam black tea or the delicate and flowery subtleties of a high-mountain oolong, every variety of tea presents its distinct flavor profile waiting to be discovered. Exploring the rich tapestry of single-origin teas is the first step in experimenting with diverse flavors. This means going beyond the familiar landscape that many people are accustomed to. The palate will recognize the intricacies and complexities unique to each variety of tea if you embark on a tasting trip that covers the entire spectrum of tea categories, including black, green, white, oolong, and pu-erh.

The world of botanicals, herbs, spices, and fruits beckons, offering an enormous palette for creating individual blends. This world extends beyond the domain of pure teas. Infusing your teas with dried lavender for a soothing floral note, cinnamon for a warm and spicy kick, or dried citrus peels for a zesty twist is something you might consider as an option. Freshness and depth can be added to a dish using mint, chamomile, and lemongrass. On the other hand, sweetness and complexity can be added by using fruits such as berries, apples, or tropical types. The choices are as limitless as your imagination, and they invite you to compose a symphony of flavors that are in tune with your preferences in terms of taste.

The practice of tea blending, an artistic creation that combines various types of tea and botanicals, enables an infinite amount of experimenting with varied flavor profiles. To create infusions that are harmonious and well-balanced, you should take on the role of a tea alchemist and combine base teas with components that are either complementary or contrasting to one another. For instance, you might make a traditional Earl Grey by combining a robust black tea with the zesty notes of bergamot. Alternatively, you can create a fragrant and delicate floral blend by combining a calm white tea with jasmine blossoms. The key to successful blending is to be thoroughly aware of each component's flavor profiles and to allow them to interact synergistically.

When experimenting with different tea flavors, culinary creativity can serve as a guiding force. When we draw parallels between the world of tea and the art of cooking, we expand the range of options available. Consider the concepts of flavor pairing that chefs use to create well-balanced dishes. An excellent combination reminiscent of a dessert can be achieved by combining the sweet and floral notes of jasmine green tea with an herbal blend naturally infused with honey. Experiment with savory components by infusing teas with rosemary, thyme, or basil. This will create one-of-a-kind and delicious tea blends that push the boundaries of what is traditionally expected.

Experimentation is not just about blending different ingredients but also about exploring alternative brewing procedures. This is where the joy of experimentation lies. The water temperature, the amount of time spent steeping the tea, and the brewing vessels all produce significantly different flavor profiles from the same tea or mix. Explore the possibility of highlighting particular notes by experimenting with different temperatures. For example, you can use cooler temperatures to preserve delicate nuances and warmer temperatures to extract intense flavors. You may manage the intensity of the brew by adjusting the steeping times, allowing you to achieve either a delicate infusion or a robust, full-bodied cup of coffee. There are a variety of brewing containers that can be used to impact the flavor, fragrance, and mouthfeel of tea. These vessels include teapots, gaiwans, and even odd possibilities such as French presses.

The infusion of creativity extends to the art of tea mocktails and culinary pairings, where teas become the critical ingredient in the composition of non-alcoholic beverages and the enhancement of the dining experience. To make iced teas that are delightful and highlight the inherent sweetness of the leaves without containing any bitterness, you should experiment with different cold brewing processes. Creating effervescent and alcohol-free tea spritzers can be accomplished by infusing teas with fruits, herbs, or spices and then having them paired with sparkling water. You may take the experience of drinking tea to a higher level by pairing particular blends with food and allowing the flavors to complement or contrast with the dish's components. For instance, a floral Jasmine Pearl green tea could complement light salads or shellfish, while a smokey Lapsang Souchong could be the ideal beverage to combine with grilled meats.

Inviting tea enthusiasts to become active participants in their tea journey and establishing a deeper connection with the brewing process can be accomplished by embracing the world of tea as a canvas for flavor experimentation. Experimenting with various flavors will allow you to engage your senses in exploring fragrances, colors, and tastes. Consider keeping a tea journal to record your discoveries as you engage in taste experimentation. In this notebook, you will record your materials, the brewing parameters, and your tasting impressions. You can refine your preferences, revisit effective combinations, and keep track of your growing palette with the help of this diary, which will become an invaluable resource.

Not only does experimenting with different flavors in tea involve the creation of delectable infusions, but it also involves cultivating a sense of attention and presence. Engage in the ritual of preparing tea as a meditation, allowing the fragrances to drift and the colors to unfold as you move through each process step. The overall experience of drinking tea is elevated by this attentive approach, which transforms the beverage into a moment of peace and introspection for the individual. As you continue to experiment and improve your favorite flavor profiles, the act of brewing becomes a self-expression. This personal ritual celebrates the individuality and creativity of your journey through the world of tea.

In response to the increased interest in taste exploration, the market has expanded the variety of artisanal and flavored teas offered to consumers. These teas frequently have carefully designed blends that use fruits, flowers, herbs, and spices to produce unique and fascinating flavor combinations. The genuine essence of experimentation resides in the hands-on process of blending and infusing teas at home. While discovering commercially available flavored teas can be a convenient method to explore new tastes, the true essence of experimentation lies in producing teas at home. By taking an active role in making your blends, you will acquire a more profound comprehension of the dynamics of flavor and the interaction of ingredients, which will, in turn, create a sense of empowerment and inventiveness in your journey through the world of tea.

It is crucial to approach the flavor testing process with an open mind and a readiness to embrace the unexpected as you venture into flavor exploration. Not every combination may result in a particular favorite; however, each attempt will contribute to your awareness of flavors, your preferences regarding your palate, and the ability to blend tea artistically. Each cup of tea represents a new chapter in your ongoing tea tale, and the trip is all about discovering new things about yourself and getting to know yourself better. The world of tea awaits you with various tastes that will stir your curiosity and inspire your creativity. Whether you find joy in the simplicity of a single-origin tea or revel in the intricacy of your skillfully prepared blends, the world of tea is waiting for you.

Creating Your Signature Tea Blend

In the expansive realm of tea, where diversity reigns supreme, enthusiasts often find themselves drawn to the exquisite nuances of single-origin brews and the enticing prospect of crafting a unique and personalized tea blend. I invite you to become an alchemist of flavors and scents. Creating your tea mix is a voyage that goes beyond the limitations of standard brewing. The purpose of this section is to delve into the art of building your tea blend and the joy that comes with it. It will delve into the complexities, techniques, and the profound satisfaction of infusing a cup of tea with your creative essence.

The cornerstone of any signature blend is a profound comprehension of the different components that contribute to the overall flavor profile of the blend. It would help if you first became acquainted with several other teas to start your adventure. It would help if you investigated the qualities of black, green, white, oolong, and pu-erh teas. The malty richness of black teas and the delicate and flowery notes of white teas are only two examples of the distinctive qualities that are brought about by each various type of tea. Explore the world of herbs, spices, and botanicals by experimenting with multiple substances such as chamomile, lavender, cinnamon, and cardamom. During the process of becoming familiar with the wide variety of elements that are accessible, it is essential to make a note of the flavors that are most prevalent in your preferences.

At the core of creating a distinctive blend is the synergy between various types of tea and ingredients that are complementary or opposing to one another. The first step is to choose a base tea that will act as the canvas for your artwork. If you decide to go with the boldness of a black tea, the freshness of a green tea, or the depth of oolong, the base tea is the one that determines the overall flavor profile of the blend. The flavor notes of the base tea should be taken into consideration. Is it malty, vegetal, flowery, or earthy taste? This understanding will guide your subsequent decisions in building a harmonic fusion.

After deciding on a base tea, you may prepare to go on the journey of stacking flavors. The natural qualities of the primary tea are enhanced by the addition of complementary ingredients, resulting in a well-rounded and balanced mix for consumption. If you have chosen a robust black tea, for instance, you might want to infuse it with dried fruits such as berries or apricots to impart a hint of sweetness and a sense of color. If you are dealing with green tea, you can add herbs such as mint or lemongrass to give the beverage a hint of citrus and a sense of freshness. It is essential to allow each component to shine while simultaneously contributing to the delicious symphony that is the whole.

On the other hand, combining aspects that contrast one another might give your blend more depth and complexity. Imagine the earthy richness of pu-erh combined with the spicy warmth of ginger or the flowery notes of jasmine combined with the citrusy zing of bergamot. Both of these combinations would be fascinating. Tastes opposing one another provide a dynamic interplay on the tongue, providing a multi-layered experience with every sip. Establishing that delicate balance where neither the base tea nor the additional components overpower one another but instead integrate into a harmonious fusion is the skill that lies in the process of establishing that balance.

When creating a distinctive blend, experimentation is at the core of the process, and the journey is characterized by a willingness to take risks and accept unexpected ingredient combinations. Let your curiosity direct your choices, and don't be afraid to push the boundaries of what is considered a conventional match. Please take into consideration the possibility of combining teas with unorthodox components, such as a black tea that has been infused with rosemary or a green tea that has features of saffron entwined with it. The opportunity to experiment with and establish your particular preferences in terms of flavor is one of the most attractive aspects of making your signature blend.

While engaging in the hands-on process of blending, it is essential to remember that the art of producing a signature tea blend requires not only the selection of materials but also an awareness of the process of brewing the tea. It may be necessary to use particular brewing parameters for various teas and botanicals to expose their entire range of flavors. To find the perfect mix that brings out the intricacies of your blend, you need to experiment with different water temperatures, infusion times, and ratios. It is essential to consider the vessel used for brewing, whether a traditional teapot, a gaiwan, or even a modern infuser, because it can affect the flavors extracted and the entire experience.

Blending becomes a type of self-expression, encompassing your taste preferences, mood, and creativity in a single cup of coffee. Blending is a form of beverage preparation. In the process of creating your distinctive mix, take into consideration the event or the experience you wish to have. Have you ever imagined a beverage that would be soothing and reassuring on a gloomy day or perhaps a beverage that would be energizing and refreshing on a bright and sunny afternoon? To create a sensory experience that is in sync with the present moment, the setting in which you intend to drink your mix might be a source of inspiration for selecting ingredients.

As you embark on developing your trademark blend, keeping a tea notebook can be a beneficial companion. Keep a record of your trials, including specifics on the ingredients you used, the parameters of the brewing process, and your tasting impressions. The information in this record will become a treasure trove of insights, enabling you to improve your recipes, revisit successful combinations, and monitor the development of your palate. Over time, your tea notebook will evolve into a record of your development as a tea blender. It will record the subtleties of your ever-changing preferences and the joyful discoveries you make.

Making a signature blend goes beyond individual experimentation; it has found a place in the expanding trend of personalized tea blends offered by specialized tea stores and online platforms. Tea lovers can frequently select base teas, flavorings, and extra ingredients through these services to create a bespoke blend that matches their preferences. The essence of making your signature tea lies in the hands-on process of experimentation, self-discovery, and the delight of witnessing your one-of-a-kind creation. While these alternatives give a simple way to access personalized blends, the value of crafting your signature tea rests in learning about yourself.

The emotional connection formed with a signature tea blend extends beyond the sensory experience; it becomes a reflection of your identity and a source of pride for you. Others can participate in the creation that encompasses your taste and ingenuity if you share your blend with your friends and family. This adds a community component to the adventure. If you want to create a one-of-a-kind and considerate present that embodies the essence of your adventure with tea, consider giving your trademark blend as a gift to the people you care about.

In conclusion, the process of developing your signature tea blend is an undertaking that is incredibly personal and fulfilling, and it successfully captures the spirit of your journey through the world of tea. You are engaging in a celebration of creativity, an exploration of flavors, and a reflection of your developing palate all at the same time. It would help if you embraced the art of blending as a self-expression as you embark on your adventure. You will allow each cup to tell a story that is uniquely yours. Creating your distinctive blend, whether intended to be a daily habit, a special treat for guests, or a treasured present, becomes a monument to the joy that can be found in the countless possibilities in the world of tea.

CHAPTER VIII

Tea Brewing Techniques

Mastering the Art of Brewing

In the world of tea, brewing is not merely a routine but a nuanced and intricate art form that, when mastered, can transform a simple infusion into a sublime experience. The art of brewing involves striking a precise balance between several aspects, including the selection of the appropriate tea and water, the honing of brewing processes, and the comprehension of the influence of time and temperature. In this section, the author looks into the numerous facets of mastering the art of brewing, bringing tea drinkers on a journey to enrich their tea experience, and unleashing the complete range of flavors, aromas, and nuances concealed inside each leaf.

The procurement of tea leaves of superior quality is the cornerstone of a truly extraordinary tea brewing process. Every variety of tea, whether it be black, green, white, oolong, or pu-erh, possesses a unique set of qualities influenced by the specific brewing techniques utilized. The quality of the leaves determines how the entire brewing process is carried out. This is true regardless of whether you opt for the malty depth of an Assam black tea, the grassy notes of a Japanese green tea, or the floral complexity of an oolong. Anyone who aspires to become a tea connoisseur should try out a wide range of single-origin teas. This will allow their palates to recognize each tea's distinctive characteristics and uncover their favorites.

In brewing, water, sometimes disregarded despite its importance, plays a critical role. The final infusion is substantially influenced by the quality of the water, its mineral content, and temperature. In an ideal scenario, the natural tastes of the tea are enhanced by using fresh and filtered water devoid of any pollutants. Green teas may prefer cooler water temperatures to preserve delicate notes, while black teas typically benefit from hotter temperatures to extract robust tastes. Different teas achieve different levels of success when it comes to water temperatures. To become an expert in brewing, it is essential to have a solid understanding of the link between the water quality, temperature, and the type of tea.

An extension of the process of brewing tea is the usage of teaware, which includes anything from teapots and gaiwans to infusers and teacups. It is possible to influence the brewing procedure, aroma, and even the appearance of the final cup of tea by selecting the appropriate teaware. For example, porcelain or ceramic teapots are highly regarded due to their neutrality, which enables the genuine essence of the tea to be brought out and become more apparent. Teapots made of cast iron are excellent at maintaining heat, which makes them highly suitable for specific types of tea. On the other hand, glass vessels offer a beautiful spectacle as the leaves unfold and colors appear. When tea fans investigate the many options available for teaware, they can personalize their brewing experience and learn about the subtleties that each vessel brings to the infusion.

When it comes to brewing tea, temperature control is essential since it determines how flavors and fragrances are extracted from the tea. Different kinds of tea require different water temperatures to achieve the best possible effects. Green teas, for example, are often stored at temperatures ranging from 80 to 85 degrees Celsius (or 175 to 185 degrees Fahrenheit), which helps to preserve their delicate nature. On the other hand, black teas may demand hotter water, ranging from 200 to 212 degrees Fahrenheit (93 to 100 degrees Celsius), to release their full-bodied richness. By investing in a dependable thermometer or an electric kettle that features temperature control, enthusiasts can fine-tune their brewing conditions, guaranteeing a precise and consistent experience.

When it comes to brewing, time is another crucial aspect frequently referred to as the steeping or infusion time. The time the tea leaves are allowed to come into contact with water defines the intensity of taste, the quantity of tea, and the overall personality of the infusion. Shorter steeping periods are recommended to prevent bitterness from occurring in delicate teas. On the other hand, longer steeping times are recommended for more strong teas. Through experimenting with steeping times, fans can customize the intensity of the brew to suit their individual preferences. Certain teas, exceptionally high-quality oolongs, and pu-erhs could benefit from many infusions, with each infusion revealing new taste levels with each step.

During the brewing process, it is necessary to maintain a certain level of consciousness to comprehend the impact of these particular elements. The visual clues, which include the unfolding of tea leaves, changes in color, and the development of aroma, provide insights into the progression of the infusion. The brewer can choose the best time to stop the steeping process and serve the tea by observing it as it brews, which becomes an essential component of the overall experience. The brewing process is transformed from a mechanical activity into a contemplative ritual due to this sensory engagement, which fosters a deeper connection with the artistic nature of tea.

One of the factors that contributes to the entire enjoyment of the tea is the pouring technique, which is sometimes overlooked. There is a correlation between how the tea is poured and the beverage's aeration, temperature, and presentation. Pouring the tea slowly and steadily ensures that the flavors are distributed evenly and the aroma of the tea is enhanced by the aeration that occurs when the tea falls into the cup. Pouring the tea from a greater distance will contribute to the tea becoming slightly more relaxed, which will make it more acceptable when it is consumed. Mastering the art of brewing requires several subtle yet significant aspects, including the adoption of various pouring techniques.

Learning to master the art of brewing requires an understanding of the technical aspects and an appreciation for the sensual trip that unfolds with each infusion. During the process of the dry leaves releasing their scent, you should engage your sense of smell to build up your expectations. Please take careful note of the changing scents that emerge as the leaves are reawakened by the hot water, and take a deep breath as the tea is brewed to provide its concluding fragrant symphony. It is essential to remember the visual side; the liquor's color, the leaves unfolding, and the play of light combine to produce a visual feast that enhances the experience as a whole.

The appreciation of tea comprises not only the solitary act of preparing it but also the broader context of creating an environment favorable to the beverage's attentive pleasure. Consider the atmosphere, the lighting, and even the music playing in the background. An environment that is carefully selected can help to improve the sensory experience, which in turn can encourage rest and reflection. It doesn't matter if you're sitting in a darkly lit room with ambient music or a pleasant corner flooded with natural light; the environment has a significant role in the overall enjoyment of the brewed tea.

Becoming an expert in brewing is not a one-time accomplishment but rather an ongoing process involving exploration and improvement. As you dive deeper into tea, you will come across rare and aged teas requiring a different brewing method. The art develops as you become familiar with regional brewing customs or traditional tea rituals, gaining knowledge from various cultural activities that broaden your brewing repertoire. You should approach this trip with an open mind and let each cup of tea become a canvas for your ongoing mastery of the art.

If you are interested in becoming an expert in the art of brewing, the online and offline tea community provides a plethora of materials and the opportunity to share experiences with others. You can broaden your understanding of tea by interacting with other fans, attending tea tastings, and participating in workshops. These activities allow you to share your perspectives, learn about new approaches, and acquire new knowledge. As you continue to hone your talents, the combined knowledge of the tea community will become an invaluable companion on your trip, providing you with support and motivation.

The art of brewing is a multifaceted undertaking that blends technical perfection with sensual enjoyment. In conclusion, mastering the art of brewing is a rewarding endeavor. It requires a mindful connection with the entire process of making tea, which goes beyond the mechanics of measuring tea leaves and water into the appropriate amounts. Every step, from choosing tea leaves of the highest possible quality to gaining a grasp of the subtleties of temperature and time, adds to producing a cup of tea that is above and beyond the traditional. As you embark on this journey, make sure to relish the ritual of brewing, take pleasure in the sensory symphony, and allow each cup to serve as a testament to your growing mastery of the art of tea.

Understanding Water Temperature and Steeping Times

The tea-brewing process involves a delicate balance between water temperature and steeping duration. The art of mastering these aspects turns an infusion into a tasty experience. To find the perfect cup, tea lovers must grasp how water temperature and steeping times affect different teas.

Water temperature, the silent director of the tea orchestra, extracts flavors from tea leaves. For best results, black, green, white, oolong, and pu-erh teas need a specific temperature range. Green teas flourish in calmer waters between 175 and 185°F (80 to 85°C) for their delicate nature. The mild warming brings out the tea's green and delicate flavors without harshness. However, black tea's robust flavors require hotter temperatures of 200 to 212°F (93 to 100°C) to shine. The delicate ballet of tastes in each tea kind is a symphony that only begins when the water temperature is optimum.

Controlling water temperature is crucial since even a few degrees can make a well-extracted cup bitter. Tea lovers use modern electric kettles with temperature control to perfect the brewing procedure. These kettles let you control the temperature to bring out the flavor of delicate green or powerful black tea.

Water temperature and steeping duration are vital to the brewing ballet. Steeping time controls how long tea leaves unfold, releasing flavor into the water. Tea-kind str, length, and taste preferences affect the length of this dance. Mastering steeping times is like leading the brewing orchestra's rhythm section.

A two- to three-minute sweet dance is usually plenty for delicate green teas. This fast infusion preserves the tea's flavor without bitterness. Longer steeping times may extract astringent chemicals, reducing green tea's mild flavor. With their forceful personalities, Black teas may dance for four to five minutes or longer to release their rich tannins and complex tastes.

Oolong teas' nuanced and intermediate oxidation

degrees demonstrate a diverse dance floor. Oolongs with lighter floral and fruity notes may enjoy a three-minute dance, while darker ones with roasted overtones may prefer a six-minute waltz. Knowing when to end the dance creates a harmonious balance rather than a flavor clash.

Understanding how water temperature and steeping

times affect tea kinds and variety is crucial. Consider the famous oolong Tie Guan Yin. This Chinese oolong may gracefully dance in hotter water for a more potent brew or waltz in cooler water to show off its flowery elegance. This tea's suppleness shows how competent tea brewers can dance with water temperature and steeping times.

Some teas are beautiful because they can be infused

numerous times, exposing different aspects of their nature. Exceptional oolong and pu-erh teas last multiple infusions. Each step reveals new tastes, aromas, and complexities, creating a dynamic and developing experience. This unusual trait encourages tea lovers to explore the subtleties of their favorite teas with each infusion.

The link between water temperature and steeping time

changes with tea kind and personal preference. Some like a fast, exciting dance with a shorter incline, while others choose a slow, meditative waltz. The beauty of brewing is that each tea lover may customize the dance to their taste.

Experimentation helps achieve precision. A careful study of water temperatures and steeping times reveals tea variety distinctions. These variables allow one to customize a brew to their tastes, such as highlighting green tea's flowery overtones or black tea's maltiness. Keeping a tea notebook with each brewing session's conditions helps fans find the perfect cup.

Beyond timing and temperature, the brewing dance is a sensory experience. Visual, olfactory, and gustatory components blend as tea leaves unfold and fragrances disseminate. The dance becomes a symphony as the first sip reveals the flavors' crescendo, the aroma lingers, and the liquor's color reflects the tea's journey from leaf to cup. Brewing becomes a ritual of appreciation and connection through sensory involvement.

The role of water temperature and steeping times in brewing is exploratory rather than rigorous. Traditional ceremonies like the Chinese Gongfu Cha and Japanese Chanoyu allow dancers to adjust to the tea and circumstance. Such rituals elevate tea brewing from a primary task to a profound ritual by emphasizing its attention and artistry.

Finally, water temperature and steeping times are crucial to tea brewing. The conductor orchestrates the extraction of tastes from tea leaves, and the dance's duration determines the infusion's flavor. Tea lovers become choreographers, directing each tea type through a temperature and steeping symphony.

CONCLUSION

To sum up, "Brewing Bliss: Tea Gardening Unveiled for Beginners - A Green Thumb's Guide to Growing Your Own Tea Sanctuary" is an invitation to take a life-changing trip into the world of tea enjoyment and cultivation rather than merely a guidebook. As we've gone through the chapters, which cover anything from knowing tea kinds to creating your tea sanctuary, the book acts as a thorough guide for both beginners and horticultural experts.

The book's essence is summed up in the title: crafting happiness. It goes beyond the mere act of preparing tea; it delves into the thrill of raising tea plants from seeds, creating a refuge where nature and quiet blend. The subtitle, "A Green Thumb's Guide to Growing Your Own Tea Sanctuary," expresses the idea that anyone may create a flourishing tea refuge, even those with no gardening experience.

The chapters meticulously weave through the subtleties of tea gardening, focusing on essential instruments, selecting the correct plants, suitable sites, soil preparation, and the delicate art of propagation. Every chapter serves as a springboard to lead readers to the ultimate destination. In this thriving tea sanctuary, they may experience a sense of connection with the natural world and enjoy the fruits of their labor by producing their teas.

The book fosters attention and an appreciation for the brewing process in addition to imparting knowledge. Savoring each stage of the journey, from choosing the ideal tea bushes to perfecting the brewing technique, is just as important as the final cup. Readers are left with more than just knowledge after delving into the shared wisdom; they are also inspired to transform their outside areas into peaceful tea rooms.

"Brewing Bliss" emphasizes a hands-on approach, encouraging readers to grasp the subtleties of tea gardening and to engage actively in creating their blends. It adds a personal touch to each cup of tea, turning the everyday act of boiling tea into a ritual.

This book celebrates the harmony between nature,

horticulture, and the delight of creating a personalized tea experience. "Brewing Bliss" offers a thorough guide that invites you to go out on a voyage of growth, both in the garden and within, regardless of your experience or desire to broaden your gardening skills.

Thank you for buying and reading/ listening to our book. If you found this book useful/ helpful please take a few minutes and leave a review on the platform where you purchased our book. Your feedback matters greatly to us.